READING AUTOETHNOGRAPHY

Reading Autoethnography situates autoethnographic insights within the context of two fundamental concerns of critical qualitative inquiry: justice and love.

Through philosophical engagement, it gives close readings of written passages taken from leading autoethnographers and frames the philosophical project of autoethnography as one that is both political and interpersonal. It does this to highlight how autoethnographic lessons can allow us to think through how we may achieve a flourishing for all — something that is both related to justice as it pertains to the political, and when situations are in excess of justice, related to love as it pertains to feeling at home in the world with others.

As such, this book will be of interest to those who have a burgeoning interest in autoethnography and seasoned autoethnographers alike; anyone interested in critical qualitative inquiry as a discourse promoting justice and love; and any scholar who has encountered the ethical question of: "What ought we do?"

James M. Salvo is a Lecturer at the University of Illinois at Urbana-Champaign and Wayne State University.

QUALITATIVE INQUIRY AND SOCIAL JUSTICE

Series Editors: Norman K. Denzin and Yvonna Lincoln
University of Illinois at Urbana-Champaign and Texas A&M University

Books in this series address the role of critical qualitative research in an era that cries out for emancipatory visions that move people to struggle and resist oppression. Rooted in an ethical framework that is based on human rights and social justice, the series publishes exemplary studies that advance this transformative paradigm.

Other volumes in this series include:

Ethnotheatre
Research from Page to Stage
Johnny Saldana

Pedagogy of Solidarity
Paulo Freire, Ana Maria Araujo Freire and Walter de Oliveira

Autoethnography and the Other
Unsettling Power through Utopian Performatives
Tami Spry

Ethnotheatre
Research from Page to Stage
Johnny Saldaña

Betweener Autoethnographies
A Path Towards Social Justice
Marcelo Diversi and Claudio Moreira

Globalized Nostalgia
Tourism, Heritage, and the Politics of Place
Christina Ceisel

Reading Autoethnography
Reflections on Justice and Love
James M. Salvo

For a full list of titles in this series, please visit www.routledge.com.

READING AUTOETHNOGRAPHY

Reflections on Justice and Love

James M. Salvo

NEW YORK AND LONDON

First published 2020
by Routledge
52 Vanderbilt Avenue, New York, NY 10017

and by Routledge
2 Park Square, Milton Park, Abingdon, Oxon OX14 4RN

Routledge is an imprint of the Taylor & Francis Group, an informa business

© 2020 Taylor & Francis

The right of James M. Salvo to be identified as author of this work has been asserted by him in accordance with sections 77 and 78 of the Copyright, Designs and Patents Act 1988.

All rights reserved. No part of this book may be reprinted or reproduced or utilised in any form or by any electronic, mechanical, or other means, now known or hereafter invented, including photocopying and recording, or in any information storage or retrieval system, without permission in writing from the publishers.

Trademark notice: Product or corporate names may be trademarks or registered trademarks, and are used only for identification and explanation without intent to infringe.

Library of Congress Cataloging-in-Publication Data
A catalog record for this title has been requested

ISBN: 978-1-138-74441-7 (hbk)
ISBN: 978-1-138-74442-4 (pbk)
ISBN: 978-1-315-18104-2 (ebk)

Typeset in Bembo
by Taylor & Francis Books

CONTENTS

Prefacing Through Acknowledgments		*vi*
	Introduction	1
1	Reading Autoethnography as a Method of Justice	14
2	Being-With, Home, Love	69
3	Thirteen Poems	113
4	The Discovery of Online Dating: A Happy Accident for Two Qualitative Researchers	118
References		*136*
Index		*139*

PREFACING THROUGH ACKNOWLEDGMENTS[1]

It's a sad thing to want to share something—to really, really want to share—but no one's interested. It's something else altogether when one's enthusiasm is mistaken for pretentiousness. I often feel this way about the two things that I'm most passionate about.

The first is jazz. Occasionally, I'd find people to talk to. When record stores used to be a thing, there were sometimes people. Also, when I used to go to The Empty Bottle in Chicago, there were sometimes folks there, too. It's an interesting dance we used to do. At the record store, for instance, someone might look over my shoulder and eventually open with something like, "Hey, I saw you pick up Dolphy's *Last Date* and look at it for a bit. That's a good one. Misha Mengelberg's on that. Have you checked out his newer stuff, Mengelberg's?" To which I might reply, "You like Mengelberg? He's one of my favorites! I just saw him at the Empty Bottle a few months ago. He didn't play, but the rest of the ICP was there. I did get him to sign one of my CDs, though …." Any time else, however—before I knew that it was inappropriate to have such conversations with other people—I'd just get a simultaneous sigh and eye-roll.

The second thing is philosophy. Not too long ago, I was at this conference. Some grad student was excitedly going on about Žižek in their presentation. Someone in front of me turned to the person sitting next to them. A bit too loudly, they whispered, "Remember being a grad student and wanting to prove how smart you were to everyone?" A few people within earshot laughed. Me, I thought, Wait, is that what people used to think when I did that? *I* used to go on and on about Žižek … I did get him to sign one of my CDs, though.

This is my first book. I don't know how it'll be received. In this situation, friends might tell you that you're a good writer and not to second-guess yourself. It's a good friend, though, who can say something like, "Don't worry, no one will read it." Only good friends can have the comforting sense of humor to encourage you in a genuine way. Taking ourselves too seriously, I find, is the least helpful thing. Still, as one does, I worry about what I've done here.

It's like these jazz albums that I sometimes record for myself. I play piano and guitar. A project I've been working on is to use Messiaen's modes of limited transposition to improvise over Monk tunes. To me, it just kind of makes sense. Monk used the whole tone scale, and this happens to be one of Messiaen's modes. So, why not use the other Messiaen modes to play Monk? I've posted some of my results on YouTube. They never got very many views, but maybe once or twice someone left a comment indicating how it seems like I don't know how to play. I might've deleted those videos. At any rate, all this made sense to me—combining Messiaen and Monk—because to me, they're essentially the same thing, one just swung. To me, Monk is Messiaen that swings.

Similarly, it also made sense to me to combine the explicitly philosophical and the autoethnographic, because to me, the two types of text are essentially the same thing. True, autoethnography might not have the typical form of philosophy, but its concerns are deeply philosophical. To me, autoethnography is philosophy with proper names.

I remember when I pitched all this latter stuff that made sense to me as a potential book proposal to someone who'd turn out to be a wonderfully helpful and patient commissioning editor, Hannah Shakespeare. I explained to her what I wanted to write. Generously, she said that I was innovative and that was good. I told her that it could be that, but, on the other hand, it could be that no one's ever done this before because they were wise enough to realize what a bad idea it was. I'm not sure how she knew what the perfect response to that was, but she did. I can't speak for her, but that's the moment when I considered her to be a good friend.

Another one of my good friends introduced me to autoethnography itself, although I suppose at the time, I thought of Norm as just my boss. I'm not sure when, exactly, that Norm and I became good friends. I can't think of any particular moment, and that I can't think of any particular moment suggests to me that he had been a good friend to me the whole time: I just hadn't known it. His support over the years has and continues to mean a great deal to me, but as much as it means, I'm certain that I'm missing ways in which I should be grateful. Norm is the kind of person to do nice things in secret because that's just who he is.

And when Norm introduced me to autoethnography, did he introduce me to scores of good friends that I haven't gotten to know personally? There's a way in which this can be the case. If a really good friend is someone who shares things with you even if it makes them vulnerable, then all the autoethnographers that I've read over the years are, by this criterion, good friends, too. I suppose that's the reason why I took on the project which is this possibly bad idea of a book that maybe no one will read. I feel connected to autoethnographers. I understand them to be writers who are passionate about sharing. I think their passion for sharing makes them often misunderstood. I don't know how many autoethnographers like jazz and philosophy, but the writing that they share with the world needs to be appreciated for the gift that it is. So, if one is inclined to hum the opening bars of "So What?" regarding the why of why I wrote any of this—Can't anyone just read autoethnography for themselves?—at the end of the day, I don't know that I have an answer more genuine than feeling compelled to say thanks to several good friends I don't know. Several of them aren't in this book for the reason that I ran out of time—and given more time, there wouldn't be enough space unless this were to be an extremely long book—but just because I didn't mention those autoethnographers doesn't mean that I'm not grateful. This latter sort of thank you to autoethnographers continues to feel important.

And lastly, maybe this part of the book is yet another one of my odd combinations. You typically don't see acknowledgments folded into prefaces, but it also just makes sense to me. It's economical, yes, and perhaps it's a way to get people to read acknowledgments that I myself too often skip in other books. But more than that, can we even pretend to begin without gratitude? Really, that's the most important thing. I learned that from my partner, Jasmine. I can't help but start every day being grateful that she's in the world. I feel more grateful than she needs to have morning coffee (more than, but not before then). Also, I don't know that there'd even be this book—a book which is also about home—without her. Without her, I don't know that I could've shared any of this with anyone ... I don't know, but maybe I'll put that Messiaen Monk album I made for her for her birthday up on YouTube. She had a good enough sense of humor to say that she liked it. She's supportive that way ... Boo Boo!

Note

1 I'd like to thank Maire Harris for her careful copy editing.

INTRODUCTION

Two-Hit Wonder?

Now many years ago, when I had gotten far enough along in my studies that I could consider being on the job market for the first time, I made a trip to Chicago to attend the National Communication Association (NCA) conference, primarily to go to the job fair. I walked around, not so accidentally overhearing interviews behind the portable dividers, stopping at all the open booths to talk to whomever I could. It was all pretty standard fare, but one conversation I had did stick out. The conversation started as these things typically go: I introduced myself, the person asked me what my research was about, and I responded with something vague about Jacques Lacan. But then things took an unexpected turn. The person at the booth said, "Oh, so you do representations of black women?" Confused and perhaps somewhat panicked, I found myself telling them yes. My research had nothing to do with that, but it occurred to me that there was maybe a new Black feminist book that came out that had maybe used Lacan. I didn't want to look like I wasn't up on all my readings, so I figured I'd just nod, pretend, and wing it. Winging a five-minute conversation on something you know nothing about, I learned, is much more difficult than it would initially seem. Anyway, the person steered our conversation to music videos, and over the duration of our conversation, another explanation occurred to me: This is a case of mistaken identity; the person saw the university affiliation on my name badge and mistook me for another grad student in my department whose research focused on hip-hop feminism. As I understood, she had made quite a splash at NCA that year, and that was no surprise. Her work is excellent. A few weeks later, I caught up with my friend in the grad lounge and was about to tell her my story of mistaken identity, but really just to congratulate her on a fame well-deserved. But as I was doing this, yet another explanation, this one sadly the most reasonable, occurred to me: The person at the booth thought I was doing research about Chaka Khan.

This was where I found myself over a dozen years ago. It made more sense that I was writing an entire dissertation on a one-hit-wonder music video from the 80s than what I was actually doing. Usually, dissertations are too broad in scope. This might've been the one time when a committee member would've recommended expanding one's horizons. Although maybe that's unfair to Chaka Khan. She did have that song "Tell Me Something Good." Still, the whole incident told me something else. At that point, I couldn't any longer disavow how profoundly niche and unmarketable my research had been, at least with regard to the field. With too little time left, I redrafted my entire dissertation, mostly from scratch, maybe at that point for the fourth or fifth time. Also, maybe it serves me right for never really learning to pronounce Lacan's name in the proper French way.

Over a dozen years later, this is still kind of where I find myself. For instance, over a dozen years ago minus one—at yet another conference, this time one about qualitative inquiry—I found myself speaking with a person who I regard as one of the most preeminent people who think with theory in the field. We were just talking about this and that, and then this person interrupted themselves and said, "James, I just realized that I don't know what your research is." To which I replied, "That's because I don't have any! Mostly, I just send folks emails." Jasmine, my partner, chimed in and said, "Oh, that's not true; he's kidding. Tell us all about the new book you're writing."

Now, it wasn't because I was worried that I'd be mistakenly heard as uttering Chaka Khan again, but rather almost the opposite. I was speaking to someone who I think of as a Derridian, Deleuze-and-Guattarian, new materialist. In some regards, admitting to being a Lacanian in this context would be like announcing that I was a Hatfield to a McCoy, and the conversation had been going so pleasantly. Instead, I probably decided to say something to the tune of how I was trying to give philosophical close readings to autoethnographic passages from different authors. I know I did mention the title of my book because someone nearby—someone known to me, but I don't quite remember who—said, "So you're doing an autoethnography about reading?"

I wish I could remember who asked me this. I feel like it might've been Kitrina Douglas, actually, but I'm not sure. In any case, to whomever it was, I owe a great deal. I hadn't realized the ambiguity of my title and that reading autoethnography could be taken to mean an autoethnography about reading, just as a writing autoethnography might be an autoethnography about writing itself, just as wartime autoethnography might be an autoethnography about living through wartime. At the time, however, I just made a mental note to maybe change my title, or at least somewhere in the text to disambiguate. But again, with too little time left to finish a book, at that same conference, only a year later, it occurred to me what I had been doing wrong and why I couldn't get this not-so-new book to work. I decided to redraft mostly from scratch, for actually, the idea of an autoethnography about reading is perhaps the thing that's far more interesting.

In any case, I found myself having to narrow my original scope. First of all, I couldn't believe that anyone would ever give me a book contract. After having gotten it, I figured that this might be the last time anyone would ever let me write, so I should make it really count. I think this is why I was trying to cram in everything I ever had wanted to say. One thing I wanted my possibly only book to do was to make the case for Lacan and some of the other philosophers who don't really get much attention in qualitative inquiry. There's a bunch of Foucault, Deleuze, Deleuze and Guattari, Derrida, Butler, Barad, Braidotti, and Haraway, but not a bunch of stuff that lives on my bookshelf. I like to think that some of the work that these folks have done could be worth knowing. But again, is this a sort of Hatfield and McCoy situation?

When there's Western philosophy in qualitative inquiry, it's typically among thinkers who are fairly compatible with one another. That's to be understood. People who use Western philosophy in qualitative inquiry have been careful readers and have gravitated toward ideas that gel well together. I've always thought that philosophy was important to read. Because qualitative inquirers typically come from fields outside of philosophy, the continental philosophers to which they get exposed are usually the ones who other qualitative inquirers writing from within the Western tradition write about. In that case, I had wanted to throw a few other names into the mix. I don't like to think of this in terms of wanting to pick a fight—I don't want to import and then continue the feuds between sets of philosophers—but because I like the idea of agonistic pluralism, I like to think of this as making the field more democratic inasmuch as throwing in a few other names gives us more choice and enlivens the conversation. And perhaps I'm being unfair, insinuating that liking different philosophers leads to feuds. To be sure, it could, but Jasmine and I stay together even though she mostly reads Foucault, Deleuze, Deleuze and Guattari, Derrida, Butler, Barad, Braidotti, and Haraway. Sure, we have separate bookshelves, but we do happily share the same house where all our books live.

I think wanting to do the philosopher remix had been a well-intentioned urge, but making that but one of the primary focuses of this book is perhaps too much. Really, by definition, there can be only be one primary focus. And as generosity would have it, I've been lucky enough to have been granted another book contract. This gift gives me the luxury of spacing things out. So, with the possibility of another song to sing, the present work can be more focused on reading autoethnography, ambiguity and all.

Reading Autoethnography, not Reading Autoethnography

Just because I'm having a bit of Chaka Khan-induced nostalgia, it comes to mind that when I was studying literary theory in graduate school, one of my professors—a Lacanian, incidentally—insisted that we remember that we can't psychoanalyze a published text. For one, a published text isn't the same thing as a person, and there's no need for a published text to undergo psychoanalytic treatment, for there's nothing there in the text for psychoanalysis to do any good. Most importantly, though, a published text is likely to have been edited. Edited text can't undergo psychoanalysis because all the bungled language has been edited out. It's precisely what's edited out of a text that's important for psychoanalysis. Further, who knows who's had their hand in an edited text? It could be the author, an author's friend, a peer reviewer, a copy editor, or any number of people who are involved in publication. With regard to other people, think of the influence of Gordon Lish on Raymond Carver's work as an extreme, for instance. So, if authorship weren't already a questionable thing, all the more so given how publishing works.

Why, then, were we bothering to study Lacan and read literature? We did this because we presumed that psychoanalytic insights might generate valuable readings. Literature is often rich with insights, but we have to read carefully to enjoy all that a text has to offer. Sure, you can go book a trip to Denmark and gulp down all the food at Noma as though it were McDonald's, but you'll miss all the nuances. There's a certain care concerning language that one can learn from psychoanalysis. So, do Lacanian readings of literature exist? Sure, it's just that these readings aren't the same thing as psychoanalysis.

In "Where the Wild Dreams Are: Fragments from the Spaces Between Research, Writing, Autoethnography, and Psychotherapy," Jane Speedy shares a similar insight with us regarding autoethnography:

> What I wrote in my car, outside my therapist's house, just like my actions inside her counseling room, was raw and somewhat incoherent. I do not even understand what I wrote myself yet, and it is not for your eyes. The writing I'm offering you now is carefully edited and crafted, with hindsight, to speak to both the sharp and fuzzier edges of these dimensions in my life.
>
> *(30)*

Is autoethnography the same thing as psychotherapy? Of course it isn't. The contents of psychotherapy aren't meant to be shared between anyone but an analysand and analyst. But just as importantly—at least with respect to the reader—autoethnography is carefully edited and crafted. True, what we read isn't transcribed psychotherapy, but that's not to say that when we read an autoethnography, what's written hadn't been therapeutic for the writer. Nor is this to say that for a reader identifying with what's shared in an autoethnography, such an experience isn't valuable for its evocatively affective or epiphanic insights. Autoethnography is indeed valuable for these very things.

So, if reading literature through Lacanian insights can be valuable and the writing called *autoethnography* is a rich literature worthy of careful reading, is it valuable that a Lacanian chose to write out his readings of autoethnographic literature? The value of any readings that I might have to offer weren't so much a presumption I made in writing this book, but something for which I continue to hope. Could such readings be valuable inasmuch as they could contribute to Lacanian scholarship? They could have, but in the end, I decided to bury the theory, as they say. Perhaps at a later time—maybe in the other book that I'm under contract to do—I'll do some excavation. Underneath, and only at times explicitly, there's a bunch of Lacan here and a bunch of other poststructuralist stuff that comes from people who, to some extent, are trying to glean what can be gleaned from Heidegger, gleaning such that we end up with a theory that works *against* fascism. In the writing to follow, one might see the influence of Derrida's thinking on hospitality, Nancy's reworking of *Mitsein*, or being-with, and Agamben's thoughts on community and the *oikos*, or home. Badiou makes appearances here and there also. And not to name-drop, but these are some of the thinkers that I've been thinking with. I feel that it's important to share that.

At any rate, several first drafts of this book—if it can be said that there can be more than one first if each false start counts as yet another beginning—juxtaposed my readings of autoethnographic passages along with readings of philosophical ones. And again, with not enough weeks ahead of what I wanted to be my last deadline—I was generously granted several extensions—I decided to mostly start over yet again. Why? One reason was that I wanted to avoid appearing as though I wished to supplement autoethnography with theory. In some ways, to supplement implies that something is incomplete. I never presumed autoethnography to be incomplete, but philosophically rich. For me, among the many other things that it is, autoethnography is philosophy with proper names. I don't see how anyone can write autoethnography without the kind of thinking that goes into doing philosophy. Perhaps it's more accurate to say that philosophy is just autoethnography minus all the proper names! Not the other way around, I had thought, instead, that people who are interested in philosophy should read autoethnography. Philosophy is the thing that needs supplementation, at least when it remains hopelessly abstract. But philosophy, or theory, as we sometimes say, needn't be this. For me, autoethnography puts the stories back into philosophy by reinserting narratives of people. Here, we might reflect on a passage from Stacy Holman Jones's "Living Bodies of Thought: The 'Critical' in Critical Autoethnography," one that contains an insight that's really something that undergirds my understanding of autoethnography itself as a philosophical project. For me, its importance can't be overstated:

> The students tell me the essay is moving, haunting even. They also tell me my work is theory-heavy, overtly and overly scholarly. They tell me my narrative leaves them wanting more—more stories of my experience, more

explanation of those stories, more of me. I am at once present and unavailable in my work, my words an apparition ... And then, as if on cue, someone asks the question the essay (my work, I) inevitably inspire(s)—"Why not just tell the stories? Why include all of that *theory*?"

And my reply: "Because theory is a story."

(228)

I really agree with the idea that everything that there is to be understood has a tellable story, or as Lacan was often fond of suggesting: Truth has the structure of a fiction.

It's here that I'd like to pause and suggest that autoethnographic practice goes beyond merely conveying information. Autoethnography doesn't only narrate how an author interacts with others, but is itself an interaction with readers. I know this is more complicated than I've presented it, but we'll get to that complication later. For now, let's just say that autoethnographic practice produces a text that's focused on cultivating and maintaining a constant contact between author and reader, the roles of author and reader being thus far undefined. We sometimes call this type of thing phatic communication. And while phatic communication is usually accomplished by partaking in the rules of ritual or social protocol, autoethnography does this through engagements that follow aesthetic conventions. We might think of the aesthetic as what's instrumental with regard to self-expression and self-understanding. If so, we might say that the phatic function of autoethnography makes autoethnography a unique mode of artistic scholarly discourse worthy of study not only for its *content*, but also for its *form*. Both the content and form of autoethnography contribute to self-expression and self-understanding. Throughout its development, autoethnography has successfully challenged traditional social science's commitment to write the author out in the name of objectivity. We might make a similar case for how we might on some level attempt to read the author back into texts. Autoethnography allows us to not only read the author back into texts, but gives us a way to study not just subject positions but human beings.

Still, one thing that hadn't worked about merely juxtaposing autoethnographic readings with philosophical ones is that a lot of space had to be devoted to making everything match up. First, the language of philosophers isn't always consistent. One has to give due diligence to explaining everything clearly so as not to equivocate and cause confusion when trying to show how different philosophical systems might be compatible. Second, though many autoethnographers explicitly or implicitly are influenced themselves by philosophers, they themselves often bury the theory. For instance, if I see the term *desire* in the context of an autoethnographer who's clearly influenced by Deleuze and Guattari, then I have to either make that compatible with Lacan's account of desire or show how Deleuze and Guattari's work was mostly a rejection of Lacan. All of this can be done, and it isn't that doing such a thing wouldn't be valuable—and I devoted the better part of three years minus not enough weeks to the attempt to accomplish this very thing—but the results were always cumbersome. They were cumbersome given that my main goal was to sustain arguments about justice and love as I've found them through reading autoethnography. It was perhaps better to show the story that these readings told. Further, couldn't we say that philosophical scholarship is just another name for precisely this thing that might be called a reading autoethnography? What do I mean by this? I suppose we should spend some time thinking about what autoethnography is first.

Reading Autoethnography, Only This Time Reading Autoethnography

This is a book about autoethnography. That declaration seems straightforward enough, such that one might think that there'd be little to reflect upon regarding such a statement. Its form is similar to statements such as, "This is a book about early music," or "This is an ornithological book about white-tailed swallows," or "This is a book about good architecture," or further still, "This is a book about *The Poetics of Space* from a queer perspective." But while the grammatical structure is similar to statements suchlike, to say that this is a book about autoethnography isn't, in fact, quite as straightforward. First, that this is a book *about* autoethnography positions the book as something which isn't itself an instance of autoethnography. So, if this is a book about autoethnography, and not something resulting from a practicing of autoethnography, the statement could mean either: 1. that this is a book addressing the writing *of* autoethnography, or 2. that this is a book addressing the writing *called* autoethnography. Which is it? This isn't a book about the writing of autoethnography. It isn't a methodological treatise, nor is it a how-to with regard to autoethnography. Many excellent books about autoethnography are exactly either or both, and it isn't my intention to add to this already existing literature. Rather, this is a book about the writing called autoethnography, a book that takes the writing of autoethnography as its object of inquiry. This is instead my intention, for there isn't a robust literature of this kind, and I believe that there should be.

The declaration that this book addresses the writing called autoethnography, however, is no more innocent than the initial one. Making such a declaration implies that there's a given field going by the name of *autoethnography*. But is such a field given in a straightforward way? There is, for instance, a given field called *early music*. This field is demarcated historically as that which precedes the music of the Classical era. While there may be room to think about the exact time when this period transitions into the next, the field exists insofar as there's a general scholarly agreement about approximate dates, stylistic characteristics, canonical works, and so on. In order to demarcate something as a historical field, one needs a certain consensus about the nature of what has already come to pass. To reach that agreement may not come easily, but once it's achieved, the field of study is given for the reason that we don't have to think about what the field might become. Autoethnography, however, isn't something that's already come to pass. Autoethnography is a living discipline, so if this is to be a book about autoethnography, and not to be one about what has thus far counted as autoethnography, we're left with more questions. Autoethnography hasn't exhausted all its potential. Because autoethnography isn't in this moment something that once was done, to declare that this is a book about autoethnography needs, on some level, to account for what autoethnography has the potential to be.

Furthermore, there's a given field of ornithology—albeit for different reasons than there's a field of early music—and still not for reasons we can apply to the field of autoethnography. A book about ornithology would be a book about a certain class of animals, one about white-tailed swallows being a book about a particular species. Though all birds have not yet come to pass—ornithological books aren't historical ones—the field of inquiry here can be given by stipulating that birds shall be what we call animals that have feathers, are hatched from eggs, have wings, and so on. But can we straightforwardly make a similar case for autoethnographic works? How would one develop such a taxonomy? Unlike birds in general or the white-tailed swallow in particular, autoethnographic texts aren't things that exist naturally. Autoethnographic texts are in fact something altogether different insofar as they're the result of creative activity. Their existence comes about through an act of *poiesis*. To write autoethnography is to bring something into the world that wasn't already there, to bring something into being *ex nihilo*.

We may say, perhaps, that the field is given for autoethnography were we to adhere to a poetics. This isn't quite the same as taxonomizing. Again, because there are animals that already exist that have certain characteristics, the act of taxonomizing is a *descriptive* one. We make a description drawn from birds that have been that we can apply to birds that will be. Because autoethnographies aren't natural objects, but poetic ones, the act of classifying something as autoethnographic wouldn't merely be descriptive, but *prescriptive*. Yet this book isn't a poetics for autoethnography, for as I've said, this book isn't a how-to regarding autoethnography. Still, to write about autoethnography as an object of inquiry implies a certain fidelity to a poetics. To be writing about autoethnography in the way that I am means that I've made a judgement that certain kinds of texts are autoethnographic and that others are not. By choosing exemplars as I've done, it seems that I would've had to appeal to a poetics, but which poetics?

As I've said, there already exists a substantial body of literature that speaks to the issue of how to produce a text so that it becomes classifiable as the written form that we call autoethnography, but there isn't a straightforward consensus as to what are essential, defining characteristics in terms of a poetics. For instance, the moment of epiphany that Denzin characterizes as essential is not present in all characterizations of autoethnography. So, there isn't a consensus with regard to this, but really, how could there be a consensus in general? To have come to such a consensus would limit the potential of the autoethnography to come, to assert that one has had such creative foresight so as to know what all autoethnographies will be. Such a prescribing seems to go against the creative spirit of autoethnography itself. To write a book about autoethnography, then, cannot be the same as to write a book, let's say, about how architecture ought to be. And without the possibility of a poetics proper, can one write a hermeneutics, a book giving a methodology intended for reading autoethnography? We can't really do this either. If we don't allow ourselves to limit the potential of the autoethnography to come through prescription, then how can we limit ourselves to a fixed way of interpreting any autoethnographies that are, let alone ones that aren't yet. This book, then, can't be about autoethnography in the way that a secondary work of scholarship is about another work of scholarship, a work such as one giving a reading of Bachelard from a particular worldview. Thus, more questions remain, questions we can perhaps collapse into the question of: In the first place, how can one declare that one is writing a book about autoethnography?

It may seem that we've come to a quandary making the task of writing a book about autoethnography impossible, and at that, in the space of only five paragraphs. But we can escape this quandary by seeing that with which we're left through a taking stock of that which this book cannot be.

To write a book about autoethnography can't be a historical undertaking, as with writing a book about early music. Nor can it be an empirically scientific undertaking as with writing a book about birds. It isn't a poetics, nor is it a situated hermeneutics. Of the relevant scholarly genres that remain, to write a book about autoethnography in the way that I am can only be a theoretical undertaking. True, we might've started with the declaration that this is a theoretical book about autoethnography, but to have done so straight away would leave room for the possibility of writing another kind of relevant inquiry. Given that we know this book isn't methodological, the declaration that this book about autoethnography is theoretical is a tautological statement in the manner of, "This circle is round." Because of the nature of the field, if we're to write something of scholarly value, a non-methodological book that's also not a how-to with regard to autoethnography must necessarily be a theoretical one.

To theorize about autoethnography isn't to have given a reading of autoethnography, but to read autoethnography. What's the difference? To have given a reading is to solidify an interpretation, but to read autoethnography theoretically is to read in a way that thinks and lives with the discipline. This is so because of the nature of theorizing itself. To theorize is to actively engage with knowledge, not simply to have it. For instance, I may know how to single-hand a boat, but I'm not currently on one. I may have knowledge, but I'm not actively engaging it. To have given a reading of autoethnography is to have come to knowledge and to have ceased the engagement. So, if we stop engaging with autoethnography, we've ceased to theorize. Thus, we aren't merely seeking to have knowledge of autoethnography if we continue to read it theoretically.

Because we aren't seeking to write an autoethnography when we claim only to be reading—although we'll later on complicate the possibility of making such a claim truthfully—to read autoethnography theoretically isn't to read it instrumentally. We aren't, for instance, mining the field of autoethnography for citations, nor would we be using it as a foil for our own research. Rather, it must be the case that we're actively engaging with autoethnographic knowledge for its own sake. True, to have written a reading of autoethnography may be tantamount to having given a reading, but our reading can remain theoretical so long as it isn't punctuated, so long as our reading doesn't purport to be the be-all and end-all reading, but only an initial reading meant to encourage more. This book is, so to speak, a prolegomenon. But why is engaging with autoethnographic knowledge a good in and of itself?

Engaging with autoethnographic knowledge is a good in and of itself insofar as what needs to be done in order to create an autoethnography is this type of good. What needs to be done in order to create an autoethnography is that the autoethnographer must listen to the other. Listening to the other isn't instrumental. If there's an instrumental chain of goods regarding the other, listening is where that chain terminates. In other words, we may do things with regard to the other that are of instrumental value—we do this in order that we may accomplish something else of value—but listening is the terminal value insofar as it is of the highest value with regard to the other. *If autoethnography is good because it listens, then it is good to listen to autoethnography.* This is the *why* of writing this book: Autoethnography achieves the highest good with relation to the other in listening, and if we're to listen to autoethnography itself, this would entail that we read it in a non-instrumental, theoretical way, thereby engaging with autoethnography as living knowledge. But we've gotten this far without having yet addressed what autoethnography is as a theoretical object of interest. With regard to one who reads, what is autoethnography, exactly?

To understand what it means to read autoethnography, we might look to the term itself. Let's perhaps start with Tami Spry's definition from "Performing Autoethnography: An Embodied Methodological Praxis": "Autoethnography can be defined as a self-narrative that critiques the situatedness of self with others in social contexts" (710). The self is the *auto*, the others, the *ethnos*, and between them a relationship of *with*, but how do these three things come together in the critique of a writing? To continue in this way, then, we might first ask more deeply the question of, What is the *auto-* in autoethnography? Whenever I utter something in the first person, there's a split between the I who enunciates the utterance, and the I to whom the utterance refers. Thus, because autoethnography is a written utterance, a *-graphy*, the *auto-* refers to both the writing author and the author's self who's represented in the text. But to what does the middle term refer, the *ethnos*? The ethnos of autoethnography is the people who are always implicated when one enunciates an I. Thus, autoethnography isn't simply an ethnography wherein one replaces the study of a people with a study of oneself. This is the definitional misunderstanding of those who read autoethnography as something solipsistic or self-indulgent. The term isn't, after all, *autography*. Instead, we'd be well advised to take the term *autoethnography* literally to understand the practice. Autoethnography is a writing regarding the relation of the self and people. Autoethnography is a writing regarding being-with.

And what is this being-with? Sure, for an understanding of being-with, we might look to Heidegger's concept of *Mitsein*, but our answer can't lie completely with Heidegger, for this is a term that remains not fully developed in his work. Still, for Heidegger, the *with* of being-with isn't a mere alongside of. In other words, being-with doesn't refer to individuals who exist independently alongside of other independently existing individuals. This leaves us with two possibilities: 1. being-with is a communal being, the being of a collective, or 2. being-with is a type of being wherein there's a sharing occurring among selves as within a community of people who love each other. We should dismiss the first possibility insofar as it erases the *with* of being-with. If there's a being belonging to a collective, it's a being as a whole, one wherein the parts of that whole become indistinct and faceless. That leaves us with the second possibility that being-with is a type of being wherein there's a sharing occurring among selves.

And because being-with will be a central concept, let's examine it for just a little bit more as it's taken up by Jean-Luc Nancy in *Being Singular Plural*:

> Being itself is given to us as meaning. Being does not have meaning. Being itself, the phenomenon of Being, is meaning that is, in turn, its own circulation—and we are this circulation.
>
> *(2)*

> *Being singular plural* means the essence of Being is only as coessence. In turn, coessence, or *being-with* (being-with-many), designates the essence of the *co*-, or even more so, the *co*- (the *cum*) itself in the position or guise of an essence ... This could also be put in the following way: if Being is being-with, then it is, in its being-with, the "with" that constitutes Being; the with is not simply an addition.
>
> *(30)*

What do these passages mean? From the first, we see how Nancy doesn't start from the question of the meaning of being as Heidegger does in *Being and Time*. Rather, he asserts that itself being is given to *us*—let's make note of the plural—as meaning. Meaning can't be if it isn't shared among selves, so this is why *we* are the circulation of being. And thus, being is a singular plural. There is only being as being-with, for the essence of being can only be a coessence. With-ness is essential to being, it isn't merely an accidental quality of being.

So, being-with is a sharing. I posit that there are two things shared by selves in being-with. The first thing is meaning, the second time. Now then, if autoethnography is a writing regarding being-with, it's a writing regarding: 1. the meaning shared among the self and other selves, and 2. a writing regarding time shared among the self and other selves. But here, we're getting too much ahead of the argument. In fact, we'll only fully come to this understanding of being-with after we've thoroughly examined through careful reading how it's taken up in autoethnography. And it's here that we get back to my question: Is it the case that philosophical scholarship is just another name for precisely this thing that might be called a reading autoethnography?

Who is the author and who is the reader of any piece of writing? On some level, both the author and reader are presumptions. The author presumes a reader and the reader presumes an author. Do presumed authors and readers always match up? Sometimes, but sometimes they don't. If it's the case that presumed authors and presumed readers don't always match up, then we have to say that we know that a piece of writing that's been read has been read by a person for whom there must be a presumed writer, also a person. It's just the case that the identities of both author and person don't necessarily make themselves known in the text, even if the text directly addresses either or both. So yes, implied author and implied reader are indeed people, but their identities are inaccessible with certainty if the movement is from the text outward. So, in any textual situation, it isn't that people interact with people, but that there's the mediation of presumptions that interact with each other symbolically within the space of the text, and presumably people might be on the other end of those presumptions. This really works for any sort of communication, textual or otherwise. For Lacan, this is what he means when he says in *Seminar XI*:

> The signifier, producing itself in the field of the Other, makes manifest the subject of its signification. But it functions as a signifier only to reduce the subject in question to being no more than a signifier, to petrify the subject in the same movement in which it calls the subject to function, to speak as subject.
>
> *(207)*

In other words, in the symbolic world of text, and communication in general, there are signifiers that stand in for the subject, the subject itself being but a signifier. So, if we're thinking of the speaking subject, it must be the case that there's a split between the I who speaks and the I referenced who belongs to the utterance, and this would be the case also for the subject to whom the utterance is addressed. Put more formulaically, in any sort of communication, the signifier signifies a subject for another signifier.

And what are we to make of this split subject, this I who is the speaker and the I referred to in the utterance? If this split subject is a writer, it's an always already disjointedness that I experience as a reader. But isn't this true of the reader also? The reader is but a signifier to the writer who's a person. So, as I write this, from my own perspective, there's a split you, you whoever might be reading this, you whose identity I can only presume to be as I only have access to the symbolic register as there's a me who's at my computer. But also, there's a you who's just read those words who's a person .... So, back to the question of philosophical scholarship and reading autoethnography.

Autoethnography is a writing of the *auto* and the *ethnos*. If any engagement between the *auto* and the *ethnos* regarding *graphy* is an engagement of signifiers to begin with, then any writing that does this is to some extent an autoethnography, at least according to the literal, most inclusive definition. Sure, if we insist on other criteria going into what counts as autoethnography, we could narrow the field, but in a very literal way, there's no way to write wherein my *I* doesn't engage with the reading *I's* of people who end up reading, for the writing *I* and reading *I* proper to the written are, though implied, ineluctable. Thus, if I'm writing about the utterances of autoethnographers, then I must've read them, and if I'm trying to engage with these utterances for readers that my *I* itself presumes, then why not frame my own readings of autoethnography autoethnographically, at least according to some of the conventions accepted as being the minimal incidental criteria? True, reading autoethnography isn't necessarily to write autoethnography itself, but that's only true if the reading isn't recorded on a page.

Lastly, it's not for nothing that I've been so insistent about being a Lacanian to you, whomever you are. From a Lacanian perspective, the content of the assertion that autoethnography is a way of life isn't a thing that can be avoided. From a Lacanian perspective, the most one can do, really, is pretend that if you write, you aren't always already participating in a primordial form of autoethnography. And lastly, as a Lacanian, I find it odd how some people who purport to do theory disavow the practice of autoethnography: "Autoethnography? That's not something that I'd ever be caught doing, no!" But then again, these folks aren't typically Lacanians ....

1
READING AUTOETHNOGRAPHY AS A METHOD OF JUSTICE

Qualitative Inquiry and Social Justice

Somewhere on the cover of this book and in the front matter, it's indicated that the present volume belongs to a series called *Qualitative Inquiry and Social Justice*. This indicates, then, that we'll need to address—to at least some extent—the conjunction of both qualitative inquiry and social justice. And what's the conjunction of both qualitative inquiry and social justice? Maybe it's the same thing as what's sometimes called critical qualitative inquiry. And what's that? Or posing the question more modestly, what's an essential characteristic of this thing sometimes called critical qualitative inquiry? In "Critical Qualitative Inquiry," Norman Denzin tells us that it's something that "requires an ethical framework that is rights and social justice based" (8). This all seems simple enough. This tells us that the content of this work—at least some of it—must fit within the category of something requiring an ethical framework that's both rights and social justice based. The veneer of that simplicity rubs away quickly, though.

An ethical framework that's rights and social justice based is a bit more complicated than it seems at first blush. If one stops to think about it, at least part of it seems like putting the cart before the horse. The part that leaves the horse out front is the part that's an ethical framework based on rights. An ethical framework based on rights can also go by the name of deontology. Deontology is an approach to ethics that we typically associate with Kant and contrast with utilitarianism: Say, would it be okay to buy ourselves everlasting peace if that entailed violating the rights of only one person? The good maximizing utilitarian would be quick with a yes. A strict deontologist, however, would have to say no. And because I grew up Catholic, I sometimes like to think that not even Catholic God is a strict deontologist. You don't have the possibility of messianism in deontology, at least not strictly speaking: "Shall I sacrifice my only son," God wonders, "this completely innocent and all-around nice guy to save everyone? Christ, if it's gonna save *everyone*, then yeah, I guess ...." Anyway, that's not to say that a rights-based ethical framework needs to be strictly deontological. But it is to say that critical qualitative inquiry is at least rights based to some extent.

And where do rights come from? Some rights come from justice. We'll spend more time on the concept of justice in a bit, but for now, let's just stay within etymological parameters and say that justice is something that can't be thought outside of the law. So, now we can say that to some extent, we don't have certain rights without the law. It's true that the law grants us some rights. And because I grew up watching a lot of cop shows, I know that in the US, I have something like what's spelled out in the Miranda Warning: I have the right to remain silent and to an attorney, and the Supreme Court decided that I should be informed of these rights should I ever be taken into police custody because we should remind people about the rights they get through the Fifth Amendment, and further, we don't have to say anything to cops without a lawyer present. This is the law, and the law gives me these rights, at least if I'm a citizen of the US. If I'm not, then it could be another story. For instance, when Jesus was taken before Pontius Pilate who asked him if he were the King of the Jews, it wouldn't have made a lick of difference were Jesus to reply, "I want my lawyer." I grew up Catholic *and* watched a lot of cop shows. But then again, it could be that there are rights that I have not by virtue of being a citizen of a particular place—a particular *polis*, if you will—but by virtue of my being human. In fact, it's apparently this sort of human rights that critical qualitative inquiry presumes. Denzin prefaces the sentence I quoted above with this: "This paradigm is firmly rooted in a human rights agenda" (8).

Okay, so far so good. Critical qualitative inquiry requires an ethical framework that's deontological in the sense that it's firmly rooted—with the possibility of not being strictly deontological—in universal human rights. This means that critical qualitative inquiry must adhere to the idea that there's at least something universal in the human that goes beyond the particulars of circumstantial identity inasmuch as all humans have a set of rights that are the same. But here's where it gets tricky. It gets tricky for several reasons, but let's show one way by thinking about the project of decolonization.

How might we categorize a project that's: 1. qualitative, 2. presumes that there's such a thing as universal human rights, and 3. wants to partake in decolonization? By the first two things, we might call this critical qualitative research, and perhaps one thinks that the third part of the project is compatible with the first two. However, for anyone who: 1. takes what Eve Tuck and K. Wayne Yang say in their article, "Decolonization Is Not a Metaphor" literally, and we should because the title asks us to, and 2. agrees that decolonization isn't, in fact, a metaphor, the second part of this project is incompatible with the third. At the beginning of their article, after two epigraphs by Franz Fanon—who was an anti-colonialist, anti-essentialist Lacanian, incidentally—Tuck and Yang assert that:

> Decolonization, which we assert is a distinct project from other civil and human rights-based social justice projects, is far too often subsumed into the directives of these projects, with no regard for how decolonization wants something different than those forms of justice.
>
> *(2)*

They go on to write that "there are parts of the decolonization project that are not easily absorbed by human rights or civil rights based approaches to educational equity" (3). So, if we apply this broadly beyond the field of education, as the article does, we're told that there's something about decolonization that resists both human rights and civil rights-based approaches. Tuck and Yang add to this definition making explicit reference to land:

> Though the details are not fixed or agreed upon, in our view, decolonization in the settler colonial context must involve the repatriation of land simultaneous to the recognition of how land and relations to land have always already been differently understood and enacted; that is, all of the land, and not just symbolically. This is precisely why decolonization is necessarily unsettling, especially across lines of solidarity.
>
> *(7)*

Further, regarding land and turning to an analysis of the Occupy movement, Tuck and Yang write:

> For social justice movements, like Occupy, to truly aspire to decolonization non-metaphorically, they would impoverish, not enrich, the 99%+ settler population of the United States. Decolonization eliminates settler property rights and settler sovereignty. It requires the abolition of land as property and upholds the sovereignty of Native land and people.
>
> *(26)*

And it's here that we get a sense of the literal, non-metaphorical project of decolonization. Decolonization is literally a project of unsettling. Anyone who can be said to be a settler would no longer have property rights. Tuck and Yang reiterate the point that decolonization isn't a metaphor clearly at the end of the article: "Decolonization offers a different perspective to human and civil rights based approaches to justice, an unsettling one, rather than a complementary one. Decolonization is not an 'and'. It is an elsewhere" (36). Thus, to literally take up a project of decolonization would be to call for the unsettling of settlers. To literally unsettle settlers, they'd have to be located to places other than stolen land.

I think we can agree that the beginning of settler colonialism is at least one generation in the past and continues to this day. If that's so, then the category of settlers must include the offspring of settler colonizers. Thus, decolonization calls for the offspring of settler colonizers to be in a place other than on land that had been stolen. Again, decolonization would have it such that settlers so defined would have their property rights eliminated. If this is the case, then where should these settlers go? According to the project of decolonization, at least how Tuck and Yang conceive of it—and I see no reason to disagree with their definition—the answer is anywhere that isn't stolen land, or as they put it, "elsewhere."

As a thinker who's guided by fairness, I want to take absolutely seriously the questions posed by projects such as the one of decolonization as described by Tuck and Yang. If we see the project of decolonization as a choiceworthy pursuit, then to move Tuck and Yang's version of decolonization forward, this either asks us to figure out an elsewhere for the settler or to find an alternative way of decolonization, one that's also not metaphorical, but different. If alternatives are off the table, then that means that until we figure out where this elsewhere may be, then the offspring of settlers have no right to the place into which they were born. Thus, they're as of yet without the right to a home. And without this right, until they're welcomed in an elsewhere, then they can't be at home anywhere in the world. If there can exist at least one person who has no right to a home, then it must be the case that having a home isn't a universal human right. As Tuck and Yang suggest, this is how at least some parts of the project of decolonization can't be easily absorbed by human rights or civil rights-based approaches. The concern here isn't so much leaning toward the side of distributive justice, but retributive justice. Human rights and civil rights projects often lean the other way. Now, none of this is necessarily to say that no universal human rights exist at all, but notwithstanding, to say that it can be the case that no rights are necessarily violated if someone finds themselves without the right to have a place to be in the world, then that's still really something. But this is only one of the reasons why all this is tricky. Still, it's one of the reasons why I feel that it's important to consider home as a concept. Autoethnography has done this well, and we can learn much from its epiphanies regarding the matter. And to foreshadow for the reader where all this is going, I eventually explore thinking of home and being from not in terms of being from a place, but in terms of being from a time while being through being-with. Again, I don't disagree with Tuck and Yang about what they say decolonization is, but thinking of home as a time in which we exist rather than as a place allows us to think beyond property itself, something which I think is always an impasse with regard to any attempts to address the issue of sovereignty in general. Further, I think that it's philosophers of Indigenous epistemologies, the postcolonial, and the post-structural who lead us to this conclusion through their challenges to traditional ways of Western thinking.

But again, what else is tricky and not so simple about the requirement of an ethical framework that's both rights and social justice-based? An ethical framework that's rights-based: okay. An ethical framework that's social justice-based: complicated. Here's where it seems like the cart is before the horse. Indeed, it is, but we'll eventually find out that this particular horse can push. But let's not get ahead of ourselves.

There's something counterintuitive about an ethical framework that's based upon social justice: Is ethics based on justice, on something that we can't think outside of the law? Doesn't it seem like it's justice that should be based on a deontological ethics starting from a foundational presumption of the existence of universal human rights? And further, when rights aren't necessarily universal, but belonging to particular sets of people, shouldn't these rights for particulars at least be determined through rationally informed ethical principles? For instance, should women have reproductive health rights? I say yes, of course. It's unethical not to because it makes no sense that they shouldn't. Like I said, I only grew up Catholic, growing up but also quickly out. Still, women's reproductive health rights aren't the law in some places. In these places, as justice would have it—etymologically something that we can't think outside of the law—an unborn fetus with a heartbeat is a murderable person. I think this is nonsense, and it doesn't really even make sense from an ethical standpoint even were a fetus to have personhood, but in some places, such as in the great state of Georgia—great in terms of "Make America Great Again"—this is the law. Should a woman from this state go to prison for ten years should she have an abortion? I think this, too, would be unethical, but I can't deny that it's the law. This is to say that I think there are laws that are unethical and not rationally informed, so there's no necessary connection between justice and the ethical if you base your ethical framework on what's considered to be irrational justice. Again, I think this fetal heartbeat version of justice is unethical because it's so terribly irrational, so why would I base my ethical framework on something like that?

Now, it might be easier to think that we should've just said that justice should be based on an ethical framework, but where we started is actually also correct. It's just that to understand how takes some explanation. It's an explanation that extends over the rest of this book, actually. Let's start this explanation by speaking in more detail about justice itself.

Justice

We began by defining justice most broadly as something that can't be thought outside of the law. The law of which we're speaking is the law of a governing constitution. Again, we have etymological reason to think of justice as being unthinkable outside of the law, but we should also make this distinction because it helps us separate justice from both ethics and love. And while we shouldn't conflate any of these things, we should note that we'll have to show how all three are related. For now, let's say that it's best when justice emerges from the ethical. We're leaving in suspense that from which ethics emerges, but we can only get to that later (as I here perhaps teaser trailer the sequel). Further, let's say that justice and love can both be good, but that when justice emerges from ethics, the two aren't always compatible. When justice emerges from ethics, justice can't exceed what's fair. The concern of love, even when it emerges from ethics, isn't always fairness, for love is often in excess of the fair. Lastly, broadly defined, justice that seeks truth finds itself operating in the service of the truth procedure of the political. In fact, justice that seeks truth is the ideal foundation of political procedure.

We've framed the generic project of critical qualitative inquiry as being one of justice. Thus, broadly speaking, the generic project of critical qualitative inquiry would be something framed such that it: 1. can't be thought outside of the law of a constitution, 2. emerges from the ethical, and 3. inasmuch as all modes of inquiry seek truth, is in service of the truth procedure of the political. Such a framing accounts for what we've called critical qualitative inquiry. However, such an accounting doesn't exhaust all the possible forms of critical qualitative inquiry. Critical qualitative inquiry can also speak to matters of love. When qualitative inquiry has spoken on matters of love, it has been doing so through such methods as through arts-based approaches, an approach which includes among its ways the performative, the poetic, and, of course, the autoethnographic. That's what most of this book is about, actually.

It's true that the personal can be political. This has been a useful slogan around which to motivate people. However, we're at a point at which we might attend to a useful specificity regarding the personal and the political. Not all matters that should be of concern can properly be said to fit within the category of the political. When we think of democratic political procedures, for instance, these don't always apply well to interpersonal relationships. For instance, should people other than a particular set of persons who wish to enter into a romantic relationship have a say—one that carries with it the force of law—about whether or not this particular set of persons should be together? Given that this set of persons involves only consenting adults and that the relationship reasonably appears to be ethical, then no, for this is best thought of as an interpersonal matter. It's a personal matter *between* only the persons wishing to enter into a romantic relationship. It's true that this becomes a political matter if the state has made laws prohibiting certain members from entering into a romantic relationship, but it's only rightly a political matter inasmuch as laws were made to protect citizens such as children who can't give consent. It's a political matter wrongly if laws were made such that it unfairly prohibits certain sets of people from ethically entering into a consensual romantic relationship. Personal romantic relationships are, then, political matters of justice insofar as there's a concern that these relationships be fair, matters of injustice when the law allows for unfairness, but because personal romantic relationships have qualities that can be in excess of issues of fairness, giving an account of them may make it necessary to use the truth procedure of love. For instance, if someone's parent expresses strong disapproval of a potential partner who they think will be deceptive over the length of a future relationship, this really isn't a matter for the state. It's complicated, but not, properly speaking, political. At bottom, the personal can be political, but we mustn't forget that the personal isn't only political. The personal is of course also personal.

Should autoethnography be political? I see no reason why it can't be. There are, in fact, qualities of autoethnography that make it well-suited for addressing the political. For one thing, I think democracy itself requires the power of narrative and is weakened if it lacks access to this power. Still, I think it would be unnecessarily constraining to insist that autoethnography be political only. Such an insistence would exclude autoethnographies about love that are in excess of the political. Should autoethnography speak on matters of justice? Here, too, I don't see why it can't, but I want to take care to make it clear that I don't think autoethnography *must* speak to issues of justice. All autoethnography should be ethical, but justice is but one thing that can emerge from the ethical. It isn't the only thing. Clearly, love can emerge from the ethical, and ethical love isn't the same thing as ethical justice. So, where does this leave us, exactly, with regard to reading autoethnography, with regard to why we might feel that we should read it?

I think one reason we should read autoethnography is that when it's spoken on matters of love, it's given us a highly-developed philosophy on love, a philosophy that's an important supplement to philosophies that are, these days, maybe too sutured to the political. Political existence doesn't exhaust the entire being of beings seeking truth. Matters of love aren't best approached through the truth procedure of the political because love is its own truth procedure. If anything, a component of love, desire, helps us understand the sometimes inoperative parts of the political, especially when we need to account for non-rational actors. The political can't really speak to desire because it's constrained to issues of procedural governance. It's my position that political understandings of love aren't understandings of love at all. If love is in excess of justice, and the justice that seeks truth is itself ideally the foundation of political procedure, then how can the political give an account of what's in excess of it? To ask this of the political is the same as seeking to fully understand three-dimensional space only with theories regarding two dimensions. One can go in the opposite direction of understanding things on a plane from the perspective of the 3D, but not the other way around.

Again, justice can't be thought outside of the law of a constitution. We can call matters of constitutional governance political matters. There's no *polis* without a constitution, for it's only from a constitution that a *polis* comes to be. The laws in a constitution are laws that prohibit. Thus, if the *polis* comes to be through laws that are prohibitions, then the political is organized around what isn't allowed. The political tells us what we mustn't do. In order to be as inclusive as possible, the political must be minimally prohibitive. Inclusivity aside, practically speaking, constitutions must be prohibitive because they can't logically be documents of all things allowed. Everything that we wish to allow can't be imagined in a finite way, and there's no such thing as an infinite document.

Given all this possibility, then, how might autoethnography through method address issues of justice not in terms of mere prohibitions, but in terms of *shoulds*? As we've pointed out, justice and love, though separate, become intertwined, so we'll sometimes note that the two converge. And to guide us through the methods of justice, we might turn to five recommendations from Ron Pelias taken from his article, "A Story Located in 'Shoulds': Toward a Productive Future for Qualitative Inquiry."

I.

First, from Pelias's "A Story Located in 'Shoulds'":

> We should continue to fund our work with philosophical and theoretical thought, but we should not let philosophy and theory trump the power of a teller offering a narrative that demands cognitive and affective engagement ... The story, told through an assortment of dramatic, narrative, and lyric arrangements, makes its compelling case by creating space for productive consideration and potential action. In short, the story allows our lives to take form.
>
> (609)

An entry point into this piece of advice is to read it as asking that autoethnography tell interesting stories. But here, we should take *interesting* as something speaking to being-with. The interesting itself is a that which is between.

Interest

In an appendix to *The Ethnographic I*, one that lists some guidelines to editing personal narratives, one of the questions Carolyn Ellis lists asks, "Does the paper tell an interesting and evocative story?" (369). What is the object of interest? The object of our interest can be this or that, and it needn't have any characteristic other than that we're interested in it. But the object of our interest isn't as important as the interest itself. Conceptually, interest retains its characteristics regardless of what object it takes. Interest continues as it does, taking objects as it does, those objects being whatever they are. But what is interest itself? What is this thing taking an object, an object that can be alternately this or that? Is interest itself even a thing?

Etymologically, interest is a that which is between. But interest isn't a *that* which is a being. Rather it's a mode of being experienced by a being that can be concerned. Interest is, in fact, another name for this being concerned. When we're concerned, all of that which surrounds our object of concern falls away, so that only the object of our concern remains. Concern is a sifting. We sift *with* our concern. Concern describes the how of interest. Concern is thus a description of two things at once. First, it describes a sifting being. And secondly, it describes the sifted. Concern refers to the sifting and the sifted. But concern, as a how, is a process. Concern can't describe the what of interest because the what isn't a process but a quality. And this had been our question. It hadn't been how are we interested, but what is interest? The what of interest, as we said, is a that which is between. But between what?

If the object of interest can be alternately this or that, then we can't define interest through the object it takes. We can't use a moving target as point of reference. But being between is to always be between this *and* that. If there's no particular object for the sake of a definition, this becomes a problem. Further, what's on the other side of the object for this between? We might say that it's always we who have interest, but this becomes a problem, too. If interest is itself not a being, then we don't possess interest as though it were a thing. We don't have interest as I may have an orange or a lemon. We have interest only in terms of interest being a mode of our being. Thus, we can't say that we're an interested being. Such an assertion is always only incomplete. Saying that we're interested beings makes as little sense as the first half of the *cogito*. What does it mean that I think? I think isn't complete because thinking is always thinking about something. To define oneself as a thinking being always leaves us with a question. One is a thinking being thinking about what? I'm interested is similarly incomplete. With what is one interested? Just as describing oneself as a thinking thing is incomplete, so too is it incomplete to attempt to define the I who's interested as that particular type of being if one can't say in what, exactly, one has an interest.

How have we gotten ourselves into this quandary? We've gotten ourselves into this quandary because we're trying to think of a between with recourse to only one being. There's no between for the singular, but only for the plural. There must be at least two for a between. Thus, though it's correct to say that there are indeed beings with the quality of interest, these beings can't have this quality if there isn't an object that has the quality of being interesting for a being that can be concerned.

So, the process of concern doesn't describe the what because the how only occurs after the what. We start with the what of interest. We start with the that which is between. First there's interest, and when there's interest, there come to be the things that are on either side of that between. There's the interested being and the object taken by that being's interest. The interest is the cause. It's through interest that there are interested beings and objects of this interest. And it must be this. It must be the case that interest is first, for that's the only way we can avoid the quandary of a between of one. We can't have a being with interest before there's an object of that interest. The interested being and the object of interest come to be at once, and this is so because the that which is the between of interest precedes them both. Without interest, there are only beings who are bored and things that aren't of any interest. It's also herein that we see the necessary conjunction between what's of interest and what's evocative regarding Ellis's guideline phrased as a question.

The betweenness of interest is a vanishing mediator, literally. It connects things by eliminating itself as a between, because it's a between that begins. It's not a mediating between, but a connecting between. If there's a betweenness, it can also be something that surrounds the two, rather than divides. An interesting story, then can be the story of a being-with that's a particular type of ours.

(Say Together) Ours

Let's again have a look at Carolyn Ellis's *The Ethnographic I*:

ART: When Carolyn and I met, each of us was established as a single, independent person. I had my house; she had hers. She worked in her department; I worked in mine. When we made the decision to be together, we weren't completely sure what that meant. Would she move into my house; would I move into hers? Or would we create ours? ... One Sunday, I came over to plan with Carolyn my move into her house.
A: Where will I keep my clothes?
C: Well, the closets are pretty full, but I can probably make room in one of the smaller ones for some of your stuff.
A: And exactly which room did you have in mind for my office?
C: You might be able to squeeze a desk into a corner of my exercise room.
A: Suddenly, I found myself squeezed between some chairs and a wall, metaphorically expressing what I was thinking: that this would never do. We would both have to move together, create our own new space. It wouldn't be hers, nor would it be mine; it would be *(say together)* ours. The following year, we did that. (56–57)

Here, the question of being together is framed by the question of home: "When we made the decision to be together, we weren't completely sure what that meant. Would she move into my house; would I move into hers? Or would we create ours?" And by the time we get to the end of the passage, we see that the answer to being at home together isn't one person being with the other as being merely alongside of. It's neither merely reconfiguring space physically, nor is it reconfiguring space conceptually in terms of making room in what already belongs to an owning individual. Rather, there's neither a hers, nor his, but an ours, an ours that from the outset is made up of single, independent persons, persons that become a *we* by the deciding together of a consensus. But what's the nature of this we who moves together and creates its own space, this we who speaks together of an ours? Answering this question can give us insight into the nature of autoethnography itself.

Proper grammar would have us phrase the question as, Who are we? But we might also think of a *we* as a unit, so the question might also be, Who *is* we? Because it takes a logical priority, let's take up the latter question first, but rephrase it in such a way that it can be answered, namely: Who is *that* we? We should ask the question with the *that* inasmuch as the question of the identity of a *we* can't be properly answered from the perspective of the first-person plural, at least not from the outset. Before a definition is known, the question can't be answered from the perspective of a here—as in, Here we are!—but only from where a there can be perceived—Over there, there is a we. And the distance of the there isn't necessarily one that speaks to a spatial distance. In fact, the distance necessary is a temporal one, the distance of, Who will come to be that we? But why is this so? Prior to a moment of definition, a particular we can't answer the question of who that selfsame we will be as a *we* without first having been at least two individuals having a dialogue. The definition of a we can only be achieved through a consensus. The shared meaning of consensus presupposes that there has at one point been a dialogue, and the *dia-* of dialogue suggests that the words are exchanged between a two, or if words are exchanged between more than two, between sets of twos. This is all to say that were a *we* to self-define, it can't from the outset come to an answer as a fused consciousness, for no consciousness fusing exists apart from the close approximation of dialogue. There's no subjective we, only ever an intersubjective we, a we between subjects, a we whose between comes in the form of a *with*. In short, we as something that's a unit can only be a *we* through first being a *not*-we who agrees to become a no longer not-we. The unity is always only retrospective and can only occur once meaning has been shared. So, either one consciousness self-inclusively defines a we for that we, or were the we to self-define as a plural being comprised of singulars, that definition must come from the components that are yet to become a we, from a perspective necessarily outside of that we because it isn't yet that we. But this is to answer the question of we as a unity, as a we that's either counted as a singular, or counts itself as one. But what's the answer to the question, Who are we?

To come to this answer, we must first have answered the question of, Who is *that* we? Having answered that, the difference is a matter of the perspective regarding to whom the question can now be addressed. The question posed seeks an answer from a first-person plural. And now that that we has self-defined, it can now answer as a plurality. But the question itself questions the nature of how the components making up that we stand in relation to one another, for we is always only relational. There are at least two types of relations that we should explore. First, a we can be made up of a singleton I and a set of you containing at least one member. Alternatively, a we can be made up of a set of I that contains more than one. The referents of both of these definitions may be the same, but there's an important difference regarding the sense or meaning of these definitions. When a we consists of a singleton I and a set of you containing at least one member, all the members of the set of you are defined in relation to the singleton I. Put more simply, I and any of the you are taken from the perspective of one consciousness, the consciousness belonging to what's named by *I*. You is always you as such in relation to an I; you is the other of I. However, when we is I and I and I and I ..., we accounts for each member as having its own respective perspective regarding its relations to other members in the set. And it's the second definition that best describes the most correct understanding of the meaning of the *autoethno-* of autoethnography.

Autoethnography doesn't posit an I in relation to a set of you. It isn't an *auto* in relation to an *ethnos* qua people as other. Autoethnography posits I in an intersubjective relationship. The *ethnos* of autoethnography is a plurality of I. Autoethnographic writing first and foremost acknowledges that writing must be of subjects, *of* in the sense that it belongs not to a singleton I, but to a plurality. It's a writing of the I as a subject, and it's the writing of a people as a set of singular subjects that exist in and of themselves, not merely as others with respect to the writing I. In autoethnography, the autoethnographer's writing is descriptive of the relations held between an I and I and I and I .... Subtracting this relation of between I and I and I, and so on, leaves us with autobiography. In autoethnography, the writing subject and the subjects represented by the writing have the relation of a set of I that contains more than one. Though the writing may be by a particular I, the writing is written such that it belongs to the set of I that are a we. At bottom, the writing called autoethnography consists of a description of being-with. And as Pelias says above regarding an *our*, we see that Ellis is telling a story that "allows our lives to take form."

II.

Second, from Pelias's "A Story Located in 'Shoulds'", we should remember that:

> Postmodern logics are useful reminders to be suspicious of the tales we tell. We are, indeed, limited by our historical and cultural positioning, our language, and our individuality. We exist as a multiplicity of notes, some that seem to harmonize into a coherent sense of self and some that seem quite dissonant, leaving us feeling fragmented and unsettled. We should not, however, let such persuasive arguments keep us from letting readers know what we believe and how we feel at a given moment. Our intent should never be to offer the final account; instead, we should give the best account we can in our given circumstances.
>
> *(609–10)*

I think this piece of advice resonates particularly when we read autoethnographers reflecting upon their own writing practices. For instance, in reflecting upon being perceived as a peer, Inge Blockmans writes out an insight in "Encounters with the White Coat: Confessions of a Sexuality and Disability Researcher in a Wheelchair in Becoming," an insight regarding the importance of recording how we feel at a given moment:

> Interestingly, in my first draft of this paper, I had decided not to include the field note extract below, waving it away as "less important to show my growth as a researcher." Now, after my acknowledgment of my own transformation that was set about by the people who I was to transform, I cannot but confess it is the most important extract.
>
> *(173)*

Initially, not everything may seem important to the researcher in terms of how our identity comes to be informed. One may experience what one records in field notes as fragmentary, and it isn't until further reflection about who one may have become at the moment of producing an autoethnography that things fall into place. Thus, it may be the very process of writing autoethnography that can arrange these fragments. So, if autoethnography can try to bring order to the fragmented and unsettled, how might we read its method as helping to accomplish this? I believe a good place to start is in how autoethnography resists silence, resists by giving us a different economy than one of undisclosed uncertainty.

Autoethnography as a Resistance to Silence

From the perspective of the reader, the autoethnographic resists silence in a particular way. All writing, in a manner of speaking, cannot be silent. Writing, inasmuch as its material existence makes it no longer potential, cannot remain silent to a reader. When a reader reads writing, it cannot help but communicate. Even should a writer regret having written something—knowing certainly that they wouldn't now want to communicate what had been written in any present or future circumstance—all this matters not. Once the writing is written, it can communicate to all who read beyond the writer's biological death. In the realm of the symbolic, however, the author is never dead. Further, the writing of an author communicates without knowing that it communicates. For the speaker, staying silent can at some times be strategic. Once one writes, this strategy is no longer available. And when writing is published, it can communicate as publicly as a slogan painted on a building. It's for these reasons that the thoughtful writer is careful. For the thoughtful writer, what's written is written with the care of how one would choose one's words should one be condemned to repeat the same thing for all of eternity.

That writing itself resists silence in this way makes the burden of this care all the more weighty for the autoethnographer. What should one write should one choose to write something about oneself and others to whom one is close, and to write this as though one may be condemned to repeat the same thing for all eternity? The autoethnographer's burden is the burden of Nietzsche's eternal return with the added heaviness of a care toward others. And the eternal return is heavy enough on its own.

Autoethnographic writing, as every thoughtful autoethnographer knows, makes the autoethnographer vulnerable. Choosing to write in the context of this vulnerability is a choice that the thoughtful autoethnographer has necessarily carefully considered. And because no autoethnographer can be said to be thoughtful without such careful consideration, it must be the case that the thoughtful autoethnographer had good reason to make such a choice to write. What could such a reason be?

Empirical research, should it prove to document a mistake we no longer make, might only bring shame to an author, one that amounts to nothing more than to have asserted something that proves to be false. To write something of one's own being as it comes about through the being-with in relation to other beings is beyond asserting something that can be either true or false. To write of one's own being from one's own being is to share one's being. This is easier said than done. As Anjali J. Forber-Pratt writes in "'You're Going to Do What?' Challenges of Autoethnography in the Academy": The reality is, simply writing an autoethnographic account is scary. The first challenge I faced was coming to terms with exposing myself and embracing this methodology to its fullest and finding my voice (821).

We should make note of how Forber-Pratt frames the first challenge of anyone writing autoethnography. It isn't three separate challenges, but the conjunction of three challenges. In other words, the challenge is that to embrace the method of autoethnography to its fullest is to also find one's voice, which makes one exposed. To share one's own being through speaking with one's voice is to partake in the vulnerability of intimacy. Thus, to share one's own being publicly in a published work is to partake in the vulnerability of intimacy with strangers, with the strangers who might potentially read one's work.

Typically, one shares one's own being only with others to whom one is close because one trusts, and at times, this sharing of one's own being is reciprocated by the other with whom one is close. Sharing one's own being can be difficult to accomplish on its own, but that there's a possibility of reciprocation can make this easier. However, when one shares one's own being with strangers, this sharing must be assumed to be a one-way street. The writing of an autoethnographer cannot help but to communicate to anyone who reads, and should one have strategically stayed silent when encountering in person a particular person one may have found to be untrustworthy, this is no longer a possibility for the autoethnographer who's written. It's in this way that we should comprehend the significance of the choice of writing autoethnography. And because this is a thoughtful choice for the thoughtful autoethnographer, we can understand choosing to share one's own being in this way—in this way that can't remain silent—to be the choice of resisting an economy of unjust shame itself, interrupting it as a form of intervention.

Interruption

There's the between of continuity, and there's the between of interruption. Both betweens create boundaries, but boundaries of a different kind. The between of continuity creates enveloping boundaries. The between of interruption creates the boundaries between the things it touches and separates. For instance, the between belonging to the entirety of the visible spectrum of colors contains all the colors between the colors that are invisible. The boundaries are on either end of the spectrum because the betweenness of the visible spectrum envelops all the colors that are visible. However, to say that the color yellow is between red and orange is to designate the boundaries of a particular color, boundaries that touch what now must be the boundaries of colors on either side. Yellow interrupts a continuity while being part of that continuity.

And what's the between of interest to us in our own being? Again, interest is literally that which can be described as a that which is between. The everyday of our lives, the flow of the everyday, can seem boring because such a perspective on life perceives life as but a continuity. In this way, rather than passing, time seems as though it comes to a stand, for it becomes difficult to distinguish the passage of time when everything seems to be but more of the same. Our lives are, in fact, a continuity, for the between of our own being is the continuity that envelops all the moments between our birth and our death. However, there are moments interrupting this stretched continuity, and these beings between are interesting inasmuch as they're interruptions, inasmuch as they help us distinguish that things aren't in fact just more of the same. It's these interruptions that Christopher Poulos finds to be of interest in "Life, Interrupted":

> There are moments in a life when something—an insight, an epiphany, an image, a sign, a trauma, a loss, or even a shadow or an insult or a transgression (real or perceived)—seems to just "break through" into the ordinary flow of everyday life—out of nowhere, so to speak [...] Of course, sometimes, the rupture or interruption is of a different order. Or so it seems at first. Instead of epiphany, what emerges is fear, or grief, or pain, or anger—emotion just sweeps over us, and life is ... interrupted.
>
> *(323)*

The interruptions of our lives that make life interesting, the interrupting beings between, can be positive epiphanies—or rational realizations—but they can also be emotions sweeping over us. When interrupting emotions sweep over us, this alters our identity, sometimes in ways that make us re-evaluate who we are in comparison to who we once were. In the sweeping, who we were seems as though it were transformed. And it's sometimes the case that we wish to share such experiences of sweeping emotions in certain therapeutic contexts. Similarly, it's sometimes the case that in certain therapeutic contexts, we're encouraged to explore and share these sorts of interruptions. In other words, it's with regard to these interesting interruptions, these meaningful breaks in continuity, that we feel compelled to share. Isn't this, too, a form of the sharing of meaning in being-with?

The between constituting the *with* of being-with can be thought of as an interrupting between also. If to some extent a community is imagined to be a singular, then being-with is what reclaims the individuality of each singular that's an our own in the plurality of singulars that make up the community. Being-with is the interruption allowing an imagined community to be something that doesn't efface individuality. Otherwise, the community would be faceless. Being-with makes the community faceful. Being-with creates a community of plural I's. Rather than creating a singular *we*, being-with is a being that's an I + I + I, and so on. And rather than imagining a community where there's no need to share interrupting experiences because we're really not all that different, an imagining of community that would efface our individuality, don't we often wish to reassert our face, to create meaning with other I's by sharing our epiphanies, yes, but also our experiences of struggle? Can't it be that community isn't so much what comes through identification, through the insistence that what's shared is sameness, but what comes through the sharing of differences? This isn't to say that we're all absolutely different, for to assert absolute difference wouldn't result in a community. Rather, the sharing of differences seeks to share what is all at once our own, but what's all at once exemplary. To share difference is to show how what's defining of our own identity is an example, an example that's all at once singular, but universalizable into what's also singular for others who share our identity. But these things can never be punctuated so long as we live. The what that we believe and the how of what we feel, as Pelias suggests, is only something that's at a given moment. Still, there's a punctuation that would come with death. We can't write of our own death, of course, but how might we give an account of loved ones who've experienced the ultimate interruption of dying? And in this question, we should take note of the difference between being dead and being-toward-death.

Obligations to the Dead and Being-toward-death

Let's examine a passage from Joyce Hocker's, "Turning Toward Tincup: A Story of a Home Death":

> "My mother communicates that she is in desperate trouble. My brother and I have forgotten that she is in distress. A horrible feeling washes over me—how could we have forgotten that she needs us? She is somewhere else, and we must rush to help her. Then in the dream I remember that she has died and her body was cremated, so I don't know how she needs our help, although I am appalled that we have neglected her." When I awaken, my analysis tells me that Mom is stuck between two worlds and needs our help in freeing her from further responsibility. We all focused so much on my father's immediate needs after her death that I have not paused to reflect and remember her—not adequately. Whether Mom is in this cosmic place or not, *I* am stuck. I have followed the directions of my dreams as best I could for all of my adult life. This one says, "pay attention now." I have to write *her* story.
>
> *(325)*

What obligation do we have to the dead? If any, we only have the obligation of memorializing the dead. The dead have no needs as regards living, so in a sense, the most we can do for those who've died is to remember them and perhaps write their stories. The obligation of ethics is best thought of as a compulsion that we have toward comporting ourselves in such a way that's in accordance to caring for living beings, to feel compelled to care because we can't do otherwise. At least this would be the case if we keep our actions in line with deontological ethics. The *deonta-* of the deontological isn't so much duty, as it's often translated, but something like compulsion. And it's herein that we see this illustrated in the preceding passage from Joyce Hocker. Her living father's immediate needs were the point of focus because her father remained alive. The dead mother's needs aren't immediate inasmuch as the dead have no needs as such, but also because there can be nothing immediate as regards the dead as dead persons. For there to be immediacy regarding the needs of people, there must be something upon which those needs must come into contact with without mediation, something to be contacted immediately in the most literal sense. Dead persons are those who are no longer persons, so with regard to the immediate needs of persons, there's no person for whom needs can be immediate. We might have feelings of responsibility to the dead, but the haunting image is one that needs to be freed from further responsibility.

But this is to speak of our obligations to the dead in terms of what we can't not do, our obligations to those who haunt us. Here, the stories of the dead need to be spoken through us, even if that sometimes involves memorializing our own guilt and regret. But what of our obligation to those who aren't yet dead? In other words, what of our obligation to the living who are always already dying? How might we situate an ethics of storytelling in terms of not the dead, but in terms of those not yet dead? And what's the relationship of death to storytelling? For these questions, we can turn to Walter Benjamin's *Illuminations*: "Death is the sanction for everything that the storyteller can tell. He has borrowed his authority from death. In other words, his stories refer back to natural history (93).

Why is it that death is the sanction for the storyteller? The storyteller refers to natural history, or in other words, that which can be observed historically rather than empirically, which is to say that which is observed and subject to narration. Death is the sanction inasmuch as what the storyteller can narrate is that which comes before death. The narratable that comes before death is life, and inasmuch as the storyteller is living, one can only borrow authority from death, for one, by necessity, hasn't yet come to that point if one is able to tell a story. The dead, as they say—albeit in another context—tell no tales. Thus, when one is a storyteller telling stories of life borrowed from the authority of the death to come, one is making the process of dying a public matter. Why? Stories are public inasmuch as they're meant to be heard. Further, if one borrows from the authority of death, one is in this sense dying through one's debt to death. But what of making dying itself a public process by storytelling? Benjamin has more to say on this just a few paragraphs before:

> Dying was once a public process in the life of the individual, and a most exemplary one; think of the medieval pictures in which the deathbed has turned into a throne that people come toward through the wide-open doors of the dying person's house. In the course of modern times, dying has been pushed further and further out of the perceptual world of the living. It used to be that there was not a single house, hardly a single room, in which someone had not once died ... Today people live in rooms that have never been touched by death—dry dwellers of eternity; and when their end approaches, they are stowed away in sanatoria or hospitals by their heirs.
>
> *(93)*

In the most literal sense, our life is one's ownmost being as it's stretched across the time of our birth to the time of our death, our death being our ownmost possibility. When possible, if anything, one should think that we should at the very least be granted the ability to die at home, that our last moments in the world should be at home rather than not. So, why is it that we no longer die at home? Why is it that we're, as Benjamin writes, "stowed away" in places like hospitals by our heirs? If it's true that it used to be that there was no home—hardly a single room, in fact—wherein no one had died, then dying at home must've been a thing of value. And if, in the modern world, dying is pushed further and further out from the world of the living, then we might say that there's a shift in what's valued. Namely, what's valued is that the living be afforded the luxury of disavowing death to the greatest extent possible. But to be afforded this luxury, the living need to stow away the dying as though they're no longer human. The dying come to occupy the place of things that can indeed be stowed away. We're willing to pay a high cost for this. At the very least, insurance premiums are a kind of savings account for such a thing.

And it's true, no doubt, that we do stow away the dead in the box of a coffin, for our dead are the once, but no longer human. However, to stow away the *dying* is to treat the living as though they were *dead* already, to put the living in a coffin-like box. Why? This is so because there's no proper philosophical difference between the living and the dying. From the moment of our birth, we all become one of the living, but we also become one of the dying inasmuch as this is the ineluctable trajectory into which we're thrown. The condition of modern times, perhaps, is that we become beings against death, beings who disavow not only that we're all dying, but beings who wish to have no obligation to certain other living beings. How else might we explain, for instance, the disavowal *en masse* of the Anthropocene and its inevitable conclusion?

To stow away certain of us who are dying, then, is just a way in which we attempt to forgo our obligation of care regarding others. As I said, by definition, all who are living are also dying, but the dying who can be guiltlessly stowed away are colloquially known as the *dying* because they are those who are most saliently in need of care. We stow away the sick and the elderly. And while I'd grant that it's true that most homes aren't outfitted with the equipment to keep people alive, equipment that one would find in hospitals, this doesn't explain all the cases wherein we forget the existence of loved ones who are in the position of needing care. At the very least, we could keep company with those who need care, but it's often the case that we don't. A hospital might be necessary to keep those who need care alive, but when necessity makes it so, there's nothing that says a hospital can't also be a home, for one is only not at home when one is abandoned by one's loved ones. Not being at home isn't a way in which anyone should leave the world. No one should die alone, and it isn't right to visit our loved ones only when we think that they're on the very brink of death. This doesn't fulfill our obligation to the dying inasmuch as no one reasonable can argue that this would fulfill our obligation to the living, and again, the living and the dying aren't different by any philosophical stretch. It's for this reason that I find Hocker's story about a home death, as she calls it in her title, encouraging. This is a story of death and family, but foremost, it's a story about love as it should be, a love that even in its narratable imperfections, achieves a perfection in terms of completion.

III.

Third, from Pelias's "A Story Located in 'Shoulds'":

> We should continue to call on the literary in our writing, and we should ... continue to grow as creative writers. That means doing the labor to learn the craft. The same holds true for all arts-based inquiry—the better we are as artists, the more our art will offer as a research practice. The artist with the greatest range of artistic abilities can be more articulate and more complex than the artist with limited range. Craft is a necessary methodological tool. Without craft, our efforts may be appreciated by the limited few who have a stake in the story we tell, but we will be unable to create nuanced accounts that engage broader audiences.
>
> *(610)*

Let's begin to explore this suggestion of craft as it pertains to method, first through autoethnographic exemplars. Then, let's turn our attention to the craft of reading itself, something of fundamental importance if we're to be able to listen to autoethnography. We'll find that as regards our own scholarship, the recording of a reading is what we call citation. Thus, we'll end with an exploration of citational practice.

Methodological Novel

Let's examine another passage from Carolyn Ellis's *The Ethnographic I*:

Methodological novel. The incongruence, even arrogance, of juxtaposing these two words makes me smile. "Can a work be both methodological and a novel?" you might ask, and be thinking: A novel tells an evocative story of intrigue; a methodological text is a dry, how-to treatise.

(xix)

What is the method of methodology? Etymologically, a method is a way or path. Being a way, a method isn't itself a destination. The value of a method is instrumental. We value a method because it gets us to where we're going. But this is only the *hodós* of method. The *meta* of method refers to that which is along with. Thus, to partake in a method is to be along with on a path. When our concern is methodological, we're concerned with being along with on a particular path. The methodological, then, to some extent, directs its concern to a kind of being-with. We'll have more to say about this later. But for now, can a work be both methodological and a novel? It's indeed incongruous in the way that Ellis hypothetically frames it, framing it as a skeptical reader might. It's true that one can't produce a novel through methodology in the sense of how-to. To presume that there's a how-to that produces a novel is to reduce the art of producing a novel to mere technique and circumstance. Nor is it the case that the production of a novel can be repeated given the same sets of circumstances. One can't, say, go about trying to reproduce *Don Quixote* word for word not by copying the text, but by reliving the life of Cervantes. Much more challenging, would be to do this while living as oneself! But of course, this framing isn't one appropriately applied to the novel of Ellis, for Ellis isn't trying to write a methodology to produce a novel, but to write a novel which is at the same time methodological. Ellis's novel is indeed methodological, methodological inasmuch as it's a kind of writing concerned about the being-with occurring in a path. It's an evocative story also presenting us with a way. But why might one have been initially skeptical? Why might one think of a methodological text as a dry, how-to treatise?

As we mentioned, a method's value is one that's instrumental. We value a method as a way, not as a destination. But in the social sciences, isn't there often this confusion? We confuse the method as having the value of a destination, as something that's a good in and of itself. When the methodological concerns itself overmuch with its how-to, when the how-to of a methodology becomes fetishized, then not only do we value methodology inappropriately, but we become foolishly lost on the path of method. In our confusion, we become foolishly lost—foolishly, not productively—on the path because we can't see the forest, so to speak, for the view-obstructing trees. If there's a how-to of methodology, this how-to is a being along with another whose destination is a truth. We follow because we have the same destination, not because following is itself the destination. When the clearing of the way that's method becomes what we value as the destination itself, this foolish lostness is the only thing we have, for without a destination that's other than the way, the way folds in on itself, and we become enclosed by the way. To become thus enclosed by fetishizing method, I feel as though we were once told to go play in traffic, and we unquestioningly followed along. No, being enclosed by the way is to be closed off from the truth we seek. Rather than being closed off by the way, our way must be a poetic way, the creative way that brings forth *ex nihilo*, the creative way that's described by *poiesis*.

Qualitative Methods as Poiesis

Yet another passage from Carolyn Ellis's *The Ethnographic I*:

> Qualitative researchers who succeeded were the ones who formalized qualitative methods, linking them to quantitative research.
>
> *(10)*

Why should this have been, in the early days, but at any time? Perhaps we had still been too sutured to the empirical sciences when conceiving the methods for qualitative methods. If, in the empirical sciences, following an exact procedure produces results, this isn't so for qualitative methods, for the methods of qualitative methods aren't so much a technique, but, as we said, a path. A path takes us in a generic direction, but it isn't as though we have to overlap the exact footsteps of others coming before us. In fact, this is something we might seek to avoid. This is but to fetishize the how-to. Besides, partaking in a method is not to follow after, but along with. Unless we were to step on heels and toes, our footsteps can't overlap.

Qualitative methods are methods leading toward a truth pertaining to beings whose being is given over to them as meaning. The techniques of the empirical sciences fail to disclose the truth of beings of meaning because there can be no exact technique of interpretation. The methods of interpretation can't be formalized as such, for interpretation itself is what gives form to the content. Here, methods aren't as techniques, but more as style. For qualitative methods, method and style become intertwined in a mutually supportive way. While style can be the result of an adherence to technique, not all style has a technique. Style is simply that which is shaped by its instrument. In qualitative methods, our instrument is interpretation. Thus, what qualitative methods produce aren't results—results in the sense of the empirical sciences—but stylized interpretations. This is why narrative is so important to autoethnography. Narrative is an interpretation of the world. Autoethnography is a narrative interpretation of meaningful beings in the world. Narratives can't be without style, and as such, narrative methods, methods such as autoethnography, must always be uttered in a style. And because narratives aren't narratives as such without interpretation, interpretation being something that itself can't be formalized, there can be no exact technique for autoethnography.

Just as there's no exact technique for reading *The Aeneid*, there's no exact technique for reading our narratives of the world. There isn't a definitive reading of either, only ways that disclose the truths of these narratives. And though we may have applied what might be called a technique to writing our narrative of the world, the procedural technique of the sciences really isn't what's here at stake. Again, *The Aeneid* was written in the particular meter of heroic verse. However, this doesn't make Virgil a scientist, but a poet. If there are techniques to writing autoethnography, these are similarly poetic ones. It's only when the method of autoethnography becomes intertwined with the style of poetic technique, when it produces through *poiesis*, that we can say that autoethnography has properly developed as a methodology. The product of *poiesis* isn't a result, of course, but an object both of and for interpretation. This is also broadly true, I would say, for other interpretive qualitative methodologies. Still, at bottom, this suggests that autoethnography ought to be read in the same way as we interpret aesthetic works. We interpret aesthetic works with our attention toward the types of truths only aesthetic works reveal. Just as *The Aeneid* is an epic poem in dactylic hexameter, and Ellis's book is a methodological novel, autoethnography, in general, is research that's aesthetic. As such, it's doubly interesting regarding both content and form. However, how might all this apply to reading? How might we approach autoethnography as a craft from a reader's perspective? For this, we might explore the craft of reading itself, and when it comes to reading for research, we might explore the craft of citation which is but the promise to have read.

Lord of the Files

This is from Walter Benjamin's, *Selected Writings, Volume 1, 1913–1926*:

> And today the book is already, as the present mode of scholarly production demonstrates, an outdated mediation between two different filing systems. For everything that matters is to be found in the card box of the researcher who wrote it, and the scholar studying it assimilates it into his own card index.
>
> (456)

Benjamin's assertion here is the embodiment of the principle behind what I like to call charitable reading. The way in which we'll understand charitable reading here is this: When encountering a text, our interpretive aim should be one seeking the truth told by that text. While the term *charitable reading* has the most currency in the context of analytic philosophy, I like to think about it in terms of psychoanalysis. Why, for instance, is psychoanalysis interested in things such as parapraxis, in things such as slips of the tongue? Psychoanalysis is interested in such errors in speech for the reason that it believes that the truth always speaks. Put another way, it believes not just that there's truth even in error, but there's truth especially in error. While one can't psychoanalyze a text—although there's a case to be made that this is what Freud attempted to do when writing on

Schreber's *Memoirs of My Nervous Illness*—I still believe this is the best way to read, to read, so to speak, as though to collect into one's card box the epiphanic, to collect into one's card box that which leads up to the truth.

One might think that to read charitably, to read with an aim at discovering the truth of a text, would be the primary mode of scholarly reading. However, this isn't so. Take, for example, common practices with regard to the literature review.

Benjamin's Card Box over Breakfast of Champions?

If, on some level, citations are written promises to have read something, then lit reviews are full of such promises. But what sorts of promises do lit reviews tend to make? When we make promises, we typically do so for a reason. And if we've done something for a reason, then we've done it in a particular way. So, what's at stake here isn't only, *Why* read? but, To have read *how*?

Lit reviews often assert the importance or necessity of the present work, and that importance or necessity takes the form of filling in a gap in the literature: So and so do look at this or that, and some others look at this which is somewhat related, but no one does the thing that I'm about to do. In other words, lit reviews can be, on some level, promises to have read widely for the purpose of identifying a deficiency.

As was the way for many of us, this was the way I was taught to write lit reviews. But should we be promising to have read in this way? Writing lit reviews to make the claim to have read for the purpose of identifying a deficiency manages to do at least two other things: 1. claim a sort of messianic position for the present author or authors and 2. insult everyone else for not getting it right. If part of the aim of scholarly writing is to contribute to a scholarly conversation, then how we write lit reviews would be a wonderful demonstration of very bad manners. A lit review put in the context of an actual conversation would be the rough equivalent of being at a dinner party, inserting oneself into a circle of people already talking, and opening with a line such as, "Although many of you have made interesting remarks about the cheese and charcuterie platter, I've yet to hear any remarks on the wine at all, let alone ones rising to the level of a sommelier such as myself ...." And after a pause, perhaps one could add, "at a large, Midwestern university!" Shall we understand our position as scholars to be one wherein we have to try to make friends with the stipulation that we must only introduce ourselves as brash and unlikeable? If we'd like for others to read our work charitably, then it's a bad rhetorical strategy to start out by not doing the same for others. Reading the front side of articles, I sometimes think that we academics can credit ourselves for the invention of Internet trolling. At least trolls have the decency to not hide behind the facade of polite language.

Perhaps some of us wish to make a career of saying that the way we've been doing a well-established thing is wrong, and sometimes this is necessary, but this is also an all too facile way to conspicuously assert one's own intelligence over others. I don't see the point of doing that. True, maybe those of us who do see the point of doing that do so from some kind of insecurity. If so, might I suggest to those people that your presence in the space of intellectual inquiry is indeed valuable, and we can see the value of your contributions all the better when you seek truth with us and not against us. Highlighting everything that's right about a text yields the same result as crossing out everything that's wrong. We shouldn't attempt to lead by destroying the good work of others. Because you can, we mustn't.

And has the practice of reviewing the literature for the purpose of identifying a deficiency shaped our reading practices in other ways? A common way to get a piece of work rejected is to not have cited this or that person's work, and sometimes that work happens to be the reviewer's own. Knowing this and wanting to avoid rejection, perhaps we flood our lit reviews with the names of everyone we can think of who writes on something even vaguely related to our object of inquiry. In other words, contained in the citational promise of the lit review could be: Please don't reject my work because I didn't give a shout out … because I just did. And in trying to fit everyone we can think of into a cramped space, we aren't allowed to explore anything in depth. First, because we have to demonstrate familiarity with the entirety of at least the subdiscipline from within which we're writing in this very limited space, we're forced to read quickly. It isn't possible to read slowly and deeply, but it really doesn't matter that we do anyway. Sure, lit reviews at one point had the utility of collecting for the reader relevant texts, but presumably the reader has access to search engines, and listing a bunch of surnames followed by years is hardly an indication that I myself have done anything more than type something into Google Scholar. Having produced a lit review is no longer a demonstration of expertise. So, in a way, we're not only encouraged to be bad readers, we've been perhaps given the freedom to be the worst kind of readers of all: ones who don't. Here, in the context of now, the citational practices we find in lit reviews aren't necessarily promises that we know what we're talking about.

Lastly, lit reviews don't fit some types of writing. For those of us who explore literary forms, starting off from here doesn't do our texts any favors. One may have influences, and it's best that one does. We need to read so that we can pick what those influences will be. Not all influences, however, need to become citations. It's as though one were to set out to write a novel with the opening sentence: "This is a love story (Flaubert, 1856; García Márquez, 1985; Sparks, 1996)." As an aesthetic practice, we needn't make promises about our anxieties regarding repeating particular forms. It's enough to know that as far as certain forms of writing go, an original contribution is but a kind of misreading, a misreading of what comes before us. That's the best we can hope for, for this is how we create from within a tradition. We create through inexact reproduction.

★ ★ ★

This is all to say that I hope that what I've written isn't a simply book-length review of the literature. And as careful as I may try to be, to write a reading is necessarily a misreading because it only carves out one interpretation from an endless number, one interpretation which is subject to endless interpretation itself. Such is the poison and cure of writing. I do cite autoethnography, but I promise that I've done my best not to read autoethnography in any of the ways I caution against. Still, all scholarly writing is implicitly citational. All scholarly writing promises to be a reading of other texts, and scholarly writing is a practice of the craft of reading in this regard. Scholarly writing is the craft of reading for other implied readers. And should we want to be friendly to our implied readers, we need to show *how* we're reading other texts we promise to have read. Showing how we read other texts can't be accomplished through a surname and a year alone. Personally, I don't count this as citation; like stamps in one's passport for the sake of filling its pages, this is but to pad out one's bibliography. Inasmuch as one needs to be honest about one's promises—in other words, not deceptive about what's actually being promised by baiting and switching—we need to make explicit our relation to other texts. This can only be done through careful explanation of our understanding at a given moment. Name dropping doesn't amount to careful explanation. In fact, we can make clear our relation to other texts without any bibliographic conventions. Sometimes the best way to make clear our relation to other texts comes through being clear about our terminology, and sometimes when we're trying to be clear about our terminology, invoking names only confuses the matter, for the invocation of particular authors brings forth a multitude of interpretations, not all of which match up. It's not to say we shouldn't invoke names—I will, in fact—but only to say that it isn't always the clearest way to start. For instance, if I simply say, "I follow Lacan's notion of *desire*," I'm also invoking several possible interpretations of a verbatim quotation that could be made and all the other interpretations of a verbatim quotation that have been made already. Inasmuch as this is a popular term, redefined in several ways and put to use in ways just as many, perhaps it's best that I just show my relation to all these texts by articulating what I myself mean by it.

Further, I don't feel the necessity to distinguish my definitions as the correct ones by citing what I feel to be incorrect interpretations. Again, these are bad conversational manners. Why point out what you perceive to be the mistakes of others in indelible ink? Really, all we need to do is to specify what the correct understanding of a term is as it pertains to the context of one's own work alone. One does this only for the sake of being understood. Perhaps there's some safety in refusing to provide explicit definitions of one's terminology—the building blocks of one's argument—for it's more difficult for someone else to argue against one's assertions if no one can understand what those assertions are in the first place. I don't count this as a good philosophical practice, though. Good philosophy boldly signs one's name to something that could prove to be a mistake we no longer make. That can be frightening, but less so if one's focus is not upon who's right, but what's right. I think that's a good way to live in general, and I feel that this is the point of scholarly discourse in particular.

Lastly, to give respect to those whom I've read, I wish to practice slow reading, a slow reading that lets the time of memory put readings into conversation with one another. I wish to practice a reading for which one can make reading a way to feel at home, a reading that takes this sort of time.

The Time of The Eternal City and Kitchen Windows

Here, a passage from Sigmund Freud's *Civilization and Its Discontents*:

> Now let us make the fantastic supposition that Rome were not a human dwelling-place, but a mental entity with just as long and varied a past history: that is, in which nothing once constructed had perished, and all the earlier stages of development had survived alongside the latest.
>
> *(6)*

For us, what is time? The answer to our question depends upon whether we're inquiring into our immediate perception or if we're inquiring into our experience of time as memory. When we perceive, time is always the present, for the present is our always. In terms of our immediate perception, the eternal isn't the unbounded, infinite what's yet to come, but the now that it will forever be. As far as our immediate perception goes, it will, for instance, always have been the present when I ask you, "When is it?" The answer will never not be *now*. When we experience time through memory, however, time is experienced as superpositions of memories of what had been perceived as the present.

Given that I've observed no particular thing at all times, when I think of things occupying a particular space relative to other things—when I think of a place—time for me is a superposition of non-contiguous stages of becoming. For instance, I think back to the kitchen at my mom's house. The window had been a point of fascination. During childhood, stained glass flowers hung there: first one set, then eventually four. I recall that same particular window with the floral glass ornaments when the sun had shown through; at night, when the then new garage lights illuminated the bouquets with a soft glow; the time the flowers never returned when the window was replaced after an ill-conceived remodel. This is my memory of the window in the kitchen of my childhood home through time. In my memory, all the earlier stages of development survive alongside the latest. Thus, the difference of what time is for us in terms of immediate perception and memory is that there's no sense of the throughness of superposition in the former. As far as immediate perception is concerned, the time of now is what is. When we remember that thing, on the other hand, that thing is superpositioned with what it had been, superpositioned with what it's now not. At bottom, when we think of what time is for us as concerns memory, time is what gives us the capability allowing us to superpose disconnected memories of becoming things.

The kitchen window of my childhood is a personal memory of a place through time. But regarding time, what can we say of personal memories that don't pertain to places? There are, for instance, personal memories of affects, being situated in the world in a particular way, memories of things valued, enjoyments, and so on. All these things are also becomings. Just as we think of how places change through time in our memories, so, too, do our memories of non-places. And importantly, when we think of home as the time of being-with, our non-place-oriented memories of loved ones are superposed: That was the time when we hadn't yet been convinced of forever; this was the time of eating Italian ice on holiday; that was the time of eating Italian ice on not holiday, and so on. And this isn't to yet speak of memories of things that are yet to happen. What of the anticipated time of never remodeling a perfectly good Midwestern kitchen in a conspicuously out-of-place Tuscan style? What of the time when we'll no doubt need to open the kitchen window when I burn dinner? What of the time of forever eating Italian ice?

Home—if we're ever to find it—can only be a becoming, and time is what allows us to feel as though we dwell in it. Properly speaking, dwelling is never in the material of the perceived present, but a feeling, accessible through memory, of having dwelt. This includes the type of memory which is an anticipation. All this is to say that though things like non-observable quantum superposition might be mind-blowing for people like me who don't understand the math of it all, we experience the superposition of remembering as a mundane thing. This isn't to say, however, that it's always easier to comprehend becoming as it pertains to loved ones in being-with. Sometimes people are much tougher to get than math. It's nice when they aren't though!

I Guess I Saw the Arcades, Too …

What memories can be made when visiting a city! How, though, should visiting a city for but a few days be approached? Should you try to do everything there is to do? Perhaps, depending upon your goals. For instance, trying to do everything would be advisable were it your goal to most efficiently wear yourself out. This should also work well for your travel partner, and overall, because it maximizes the things you didn't really get to do, it's the best way to experience as little as possible: We didn't really get to experience this, experience that, and oh, this other thing, too! Too many times had it been that I had only wanted to visit a certain museum, there in this or that city as of yet unknown to me. Though the museum visit might've been given a place on our itinerary, I was rushed through the entirety of the collections, for there, too, it was necessary to see everything. With so much to do, who has time for such appreciative reverie? Perhaps we spent the most time waiting in line at the souvenir shop, something, in the end, worth the trouble. Who could remember such a visit otherwise? And if in the span of three weeks, one has visited most of Europe, say, then one comes away with as many meaningful experiences as one might accumulate by skimming several travel guides. If one's goal is only to be able to replace, "Yes, I know of that," with "Yes, I've been there," something which would technically be true, then perhaps something is accomplished. In any other case, however, we all know that being well-traveled isn't necessarily indicated by the number of stamps on one's passport. Maybe I liked this place, but perhaps I didn't? No, better, I think, is it to experience a few rare things that a given city has to offer, to experience those rare things fully and thoroughly, even if such things might include a parked truck in the middle of a town square selling unusually good Italian ice.

And how might one read any particular text given that there's always so much more to read? Say, perhaps, that the totality of texts in one's discipline is the equivalent of a world, each author writing in that discipline a particular nation, each piece of writing its own city. Given that the discipline is large enough, there'd be far more writing-cities than one has days in a lifetime. In 100 years, there are only 36,500 days. Typing in "Jacques Lacan" into Google Scholar—and in quotation marks, too—returns over 139,000 citations. Being well-read, of course, isn't the same thing as being well-skimmed: Maybe I liked this text, but perhaps I didn't? Here, too, a prolonged stay in just one city at a time is best. Let's always be sure to make the time for close reading—readings that are always already charitable—especially when rich texts have so much to offer. This is a good thing. I do know now that it's nice to travel with someone who feels the same way.

IV

Fourth, from Pelias's "A Story Located in 'Shoulds'":

> We should do more work speaking across identities. We have done much more work in creating space for various voices than for speaking across differing positionalities … But, if we are to engage in meaningful dialogue, if we are to create a better social world, we must learn to speak to each other across our differences.
>
> *(610)*

Let's start our exploration of speaking across difference by addressing the notion of privilege.

The Distribution of Suffering

Here's a passage from *Betweener Talk* by Marcelo Diversi and Claudio Moreira:

> "Why did you have to go to an American university to study Brazilian street children?" my friend Cláudio asked as we sat down on the curb in front of

my parents' home in Brazil. I didn't answer right away. I perceived the
question as loaded with a postcolonial critique, partially because I had been
asking myself the same question, but mostly because I was familiar with
Cláudio's incisive challenges of the arrogance with which academics construct
knowledge about oppression from the comfort of a privileged life.

(14)

How should one come to terms with the comfort of a privileged life? When it comes to limited resources, if we're to enjoy something, then that means *ipso facto* that someone else does not. For instance, there are only so many academic jobs, more jobs than there are people qualified to hold them, so that I occupy one of these positions means that someone who may be qualified to have my position doesn't have it. And it's herein that we sometimes construct for ourselves the fantasy of merit: Sure, I may be taking a position away from people who are also qualified to have my position, but I'm the most worthy because I'm the most qualified! And when this becomes an issue of desert, then if there's a most qualified, then all the others are necessarily left to occupy a position of less qualified. And then what of the particular question posed in the passage? Why must one seek the comfort of a privileged life to do good work? How do those of us who haven't reflected on it as the authors do, how do we answer without reflection? It would seem that the notion of desert would be an answer for us also: Because I'm doing something that's important, I'm worthy of comfort and privilege!

However, what the fantasy of merit—and it's always a fantasy even by measurable criteria, since choosing the criteria of merit isn't ever an innocent activity—fails to account for is that obligation of spreading around suffering. Enjoyment of limited resources isn't necessarily unfair if the suffering on the other side of the enjoyment doesn't always fall to the same people. The only way to spread around suffering is to find ways to share what can be enjoyed in an economy of limited resources. This is the challenge. To ensure that suffering doesn't remain with the same set of particular people only, it's only just that we speak across this sort of difference especially and seek peace for all to the degree that it can be achieved.

Home Is a Place When of Being at Peace

What do we mean by place? Place is a non-being, a non-being inasmuch as it's only that which describes a position at a particular instant in time. Place is thus something that can come to be occupied by objects. Objects can change their position through time, but what remains constant through time is the position. Only beings have the capacity to move, so place, because it's a non-being, is itself incapable of movement. Rather, place is that which is moved through as time progresses. But if the entirety of universe is expanding, does that mean that place itself expands along with it? Even if this were true, that expansion would have to take place *through* time, for were place itself to expand along with the overall expansive movement of the universe, this wouldn't happen in the instant. Movement as an occurrence can only occur through time. In an instant, there is no movement.

And what of home? Clearly, home isn't a non-being that describes a position at a particular instant. Home, we might then conclude, isn't a place in this sense. However, a compelling argument can't be made by merely having an overly restrictive definition with regard to a quality of the thing in question. In that light, what do we typically mean when we say that home is a place? When we think of home as a place, we're likely thinking about belonging. To have a home is to have a place in which one belongs. Thus, to say that home is a place is to be metaphorical, to take a salient quality from a literal definition and apply it to something less literal through a substitution useful with regard to bringing us to a proper understanding. So, when we think of home as a place, what we're taking from the literal definition of place is its quality of being a position. To say that home is a place is to say that when we feel at home, we're able to occupy a particular kind of position that's open to us. And just as objects occupy place, we might occupy a position that we call home. And though this isn't a full definition of home, we might say that one of home's qualities is metaphorically placed. And to fill out our definition a bit more, perhaps we could say that home is metaphorically placed inasmuch as when we feel at home, we occupy a position in which we feel we belong.

But even were we to be metaphorical, is it useful to think of home as a position we occupy? What can it mean to belong to a position, to have a particular identity for ourselves whose stability is defined through making home a territory? This might get us into feeling that my home is only my own and that home is also the place where the stranger is unwelcome. The stranger can't belong to the position which I occupy, the position that gives me my identity as one who belongs, for were the stranger to occupy the same position, the stranger wouldn't be a stranger at all, but someone with whom I feel at home with because I share my home. Someone with whom I share a home isn't a stranger at all. And though this gets us into a tautology, there's an important reason why we shouldn't think of home this way.

Welcoming the stranger into a particular position of belonging seems progressive. We let a stranger into our home in order to transform that stranger into something other than a stranger. While this looks like we "de-territorialize," so to speak, what we're actually doing is assimilating in a way that's destructive to the stranger's own identity. Because home is a placed metaphorical position tied to the identity of one who belongs, then the hospitality we show to a stranger isn't a true hospitality if that hospitality is meant to be transformative. The opening of home belonging to hospitality is necessarily a gesture that lets the stranger come as they are. To assimilate the stranger is to value the stranger only inasmuch as the stranger is one who shares our identity. In other words, "I like you so long as you're just like me." This isn't an inclusive hospitality, but yet another form of friend or enemy, something from which we're trying to move away. Like Heidegger, Carl Schmitt needs to be rethought as he, too, was a Nazi. So, how can we use another metaphor to better think of home? How can we think of home as something that doesn't welcome on the condition of transformation?

To think metaphorically, but in a different way, we might explore a gesture that we make when welcoming a stranger into our home as they come home with us for the first time. When we stand at the threshold, we often say to the stranger, "After you." What's the significance of this gesture? When we welcome someone into our home as we come home with them, the difference isn't the place that we'll soon both come to occupy. No, the place is precisely what will be shared. But that's not to say that we—myself and the stranger—should enter the home in the same way. In order that the stranger feel at home with us, a home that will not become theirs by any necessity, sharing the place isn't enough. Rather, the gesture of after you implies that the stranger comes before us. Because there's no necessary spatial orientation of a home, this positioning of beforeness is a temporal one. But why is a temporal metaphor of hospitality more useful than a spatial one?

Place lends itself to division. The divisions of mine and yours aren't useful to building the community of being-with. Even when we're welcoming of the other into our place, the fact that there's such a thing as "our" place implies that there's another place characterized by not belonging. How would we remedy this? Were we to erase all boundaries, then that either implies: 1. something that's at least vaguely colonial, as in, "All places are either mine or ours inasmuch as everything belongs only to people welcomed by me," or 2. everyone is equally welcome. The first colonial understanding of the erasing of all boundaries is clearly to be avoided. The second understanding seems good, but only inasmuch as it betrays a confusion of equating the notion of equality with the notion of fairness. Inclusivity doesn't imply equal welcome. Case in point, Nazis aren't ever welcome. Not everyone is welcome in my house … or for that matter, my backyard. And that's okay.

None of this is a claim about material, but of how we think of worlds. Spatial arrangements don't occupy the same things. The earth revolves on its axis, around the sun, the whole universe expands.

A place is what is taken to be a consistent place in relation to placed things. It's here that I'm reminded of a passage from Anandam Kavoori's "What Is Peace? Being an Autoethnographic Account of Methodological Musings From the Beach":

> For I now realize that I have been approaching the question of Peace entirely incorrectly. Peace is not the result of the sum of quantifiable factors (strong economy + good government + civil society) even if those are proximate ways to understand Peace. Nor is Peace the sum of a lifelong meditation, even if that is a window into a personal vision of Peace. Nor is Peace the

place after a violent act (even as the absence of violence is a prerequisite for *any* understanding of Peace). Rather, *Peace is an expression and experience of Place.*

(377)

Home is where we can be at peace, and if peace itself is an expression and experience of place, we can only experience the peace of being at home as a time during which, for experience is itself durational. But what is our relation of home if we think of home as a particular homeland, to the *polis* that can be a nation? What does fromness add to this where during which we can be at peace.

I'm from Upstate New York ... Fuggedaboudit!

This is taken from Kakali Bhattacharya's "The Vulnerable Academic: Personal Narratives and Strategic De/Colonizing of Academic Structures":

> Dr. S asks me about my background: "Where are you really from? I mean originally."
>
> I have played this game before. I try not to answer what he really wants to know. I am not dismissing my ethnicity, but why should the ways in which we might be ethnically different (something I cannot hide due to the physicality of being Brown) be the first point of engagement?
>
> (313)

I can sadly attest that the follow-up to my being asked about my nationality often goes something to the effect of, "My sister's nurse is Filipino. They go to our church. Do you know the Rosarios?" I'm glad that nowadays, people don't ask if we're related. That's good progress. I used to think that some people were convinced that people of color from this or that nation are part of some sort of vast network where we all know each other, but I've begun to think that this is perhaps instead an invitation to be introduced. That makes more sense, in a way. And it's only very recently that I've begun to answer the initial question of where I'm from in an expected way. I used to tell people that I was from Gary, Indiana, just outside of Chicago. I wasn't trying to be subversive as Bhattacharya describes when she deliberately thwarts the "really from," a subversion that gives me great joy, one that makes me wish I had thought to do the same on purpose. No, to answer that I'm from Gary was simply what occurred to me. When I lived on the border of Pennsylvania and New York in small rural towns, for instance, being originally from a Midwestern suburb seemed like a big deal to me. Culturally speaking, that part of the East Coast is very different from where I grew up, so I used this particular version of indicating that, "Yes, you're correct. I noticed that I'm not from here, too." No one ever wanted to introduce me to the nice person they knew from Naperville, though. In any case, such conversations typically end with how good my English is. Bhattacharya makes mention of stories like this in her article also. Although to be fair, it took me perhaps too long of a time to get over my disappointment that people from Western New York spoke in nothing sounding anything like a Brooklyn accent. That's apparently not a thing. But I've indeed been pulled into situations as Bhattacharya describes below in "Coloring Memories and Imaginations of 'Home': Crafting a De/Colonizing Autoethnography":

> An email arrives in my inbox from the new faculty orientation coordinator at my university. I see someone named Ram Prabhu has been copied on it.
> Dear Kakali,
> I am copying Ram on this email. You're both from India. I think you two should meet, as you would have a lot of things in common. Good luck.
> Robert.
>
> *(12)*

Still, Bhattacharya's question above, taken along with the account of presumed commonality, points out that not only is there an assumption about the nature of familiarity, but also one about strangeness. Not only is it that a stranger of similar national origin is assumed to be *de facto* more familiar, but the strangeness of strangers is here limited to nationality in such a way that people of different national origin are presumed to be utterly strange to each other. In fact, it's often the case that I find certain other US citizens, for instance, to be inscrutable. I once lived in a red state. But even in an academic context, why is nation so salient that the assumption isn't that to make a stranger more familiar would be to find similar areas of research? Put another way, if familiarity has to do with family, and family is related to the concept of home, why is the notion of *homeland* taken to be so literal, as though everyone from the same nation all shares a home, as though such people are all familiar, as though they're all family?

There are many conflations that lead us to make the assumptions that we do surrounding the idea of nationality. Race and nation get conflated, culture and nation, the dominant political stance of current leadership with a governed people, and so on. These conflations can pertain to the foreigner, but they pertain equally to unsorted thinking regarding one's own nation when it comes to one's own identity. Why are we thought to have a home if we're citizens of a nation? Why is the nation our home by default? This is an odd thing indeed.

Homeland

In "The Long Way Home: The Vicissitudes of Belonging and Otherness in Northeast India," Urmitapa Dutta is right that to add the concept of land to home makes it more bounded. Let's take a look at the passage:

> Home is a multifaceted concept with emotional, social, cultural, and geopolitical components but "homeland" through the addition of land has a more bounded

connotation. The geopolitical implications of homeland are far more concrete and corporeal than the emotional positionality of home. The term *homeland*, by recalling the connection to land also accentuates borders and boundaries.

(168)

If this makes the notion of home more bounded, then what's implied is that *home* is a less bounded term than *homeland*. This means that the boundaries of home are more expansive, and it must be the case that were we to demarcate that which is a homeland, then something must be excluded from what would count as home. If home is the time during which we feel at home, and this is a multifaceted concept, what could the addition of the concept of land subtract from it?

If one experiences being-with when one feels at home, then when one experiences being with regard to a homeland, then one is also being in a way that's also a being from. The question of fromness is precisely what land brings to home. Land grounds the experience of the time of being at home to a particular place. When there's place, we can't experience what we do with another in a way that can be shared in the same way we might share time.

When I share the time of feeling at home as I experience being-with, then I can experience this time with the other during the same time. This is sharing in the most absolute sense. However, I can never share a space this way when it comes to being placed. When I am placed, only I may occupy that space until I move or am moved from it. If I'm to share a space, the sharing isn't in an absolute sense, but in the sense that I'm with another or others within a space whose boundaries are defined such that the space at a given time is marked off as this space and not that. Here, if I am to be with others, it's only that I'm alongside of these others. And when homeland pertains to nation, then I'm alongside of others in the nation. If I belong to this homeland, then I experience being from this nation, and the others to whom I experience being alongside may be from this homeland or not. And it's herein that we encounter the concept of the stranger/foreigner/other. The stranger/foreigner/other is a being whose being is one of not belonging alongside of beings who belong in a space that can't be absolutely shared.

Being At Home In the World Is to Spend Time At Home

This is from Devika Chawla's *Home, Uprooted*:

> What remains "is the necessity and inevitability of a desire for a 'home' in an inhospitable world, the accompanying dangers of the desire, and the continuing need to create 'homes' for ourselves."
>
> *(28)*

Though we haven't adequately defined the world, we might move toward a definition by asking about it. Here we might ask, What's inhospitable about the world? To be hospitable is to have the ability to host, so to be inhospitable is not to have this ability. But why might we say that the world lacks the ability to host? First, to host means that one has a household that one can offer up to a guest. On some level, then, the world lacks the ability to host inasmuch as the world isn't a thing that could either offer, or for that matter have, a household. More fundamentally, the world can neither have nor offer because no things belong to the world as such. The world, we might say, is instead that which can contain a household, and in general, the world is that in which we find ourselves. Thus, when we find ourselves in the world, we find ourselves in something that contains us in the sense that it offers us nothing, but simply is the *into which* wherein to be. With respect to us, the primordial position of the world, then, is that into which we're thrown. And the nature of our being thrown is always not into anything other but a mere wherein. Being thrown into a mere wherein, we don't primordially find ourselves at home. We're thrown into the world, and we only become at home, and it's only after becoming at home in the world that the world becomes more than an into which, but a that to which we orient ourselves.

Thus, the world as a primordial wherein is inhospitable in yet another sense because at the point of our thrownness, it's what's yet to contain a home, for at the point of our thrownness we've not yet had the opportunity to become anything, let alone become at home. This is why Chawla correctly points out that there's a continuing need to create homes for ourselves. The world can't contain anything other than containingness without an act of willing on our part. For us to be at home, we must first will a home from the wherein of the world such that the world comes to contain it. But why would there be a continuing need if we've completed the project of creating a home through a willful act?

There can only be a continuing need to create *homes* for ourselves—and we should make note of the plural—if a singular home isn't satisfactory. Being at home can only refer to a temporal series. Our relation to home is one of desire, something that can't be satisfied because desire itself takes no object, but only has an object cause. Desire never ceases, because whatever it is that we're able to grasp is never actually the object, for it's desire's nature to never take an object. It's a foregone conclusion that whatever it is that we get isn't what we want. This only makes sense on a structural level: One can't want what one already has because wanting pertains to something not had. And Chawla is correct that we have a relationship of desire toward creating homes, creating homes in the inhospitable world into which we're thrown. What we see is that what we seek isn't simply to make a home in the world, but to be at home in the world. The world isn't a place into which, but a time into which.

The Not Duty of Hospitality

Let's take a look at a passage from *Of Hospitality* by Jacques Derrida:

This unconditional law of hospitality, if such a thing is thinkable, would then be a law without imperative, without order and without duty. A law without law, in short. For if I practice hospitality "out of duty" [and not only "in conforming with duty"], this hospitality of paying up is no longer an absolute hospitality, it is no longer graciously offered beyond debt and economy, offered to the other, a hospitality invented for the singularity of the new arrival, of the unexpected visitor.

(83)

Not only must one not act out of duty, but in order to be hospitable, it must first be that one can function in the capacity of a host. In other words, one must have a home that can be opened, a home into which another can be welcomed. If we think of the home as spatial, we encounter several questions regarding who has the right to be hospitable. For instance, if I'm a guest in someone else's home, do I have the right to open another's home? Can a guest as a guest be hospitable? It would seem that the answer is no, for when not at home, a guest is a guest inasmuch as they've been received into a home that isn't their own. Invitations are either absolutely open or apply only to particular persons. If a home has been opened absolutely, the guest can't open that home more. If the invitation were specific, then the implication is that that home is otherwise closed. Were a guest to try to attempt to open a home not their own, the closure remains inasmuch as from the perspective of the host, anyone other than the welcomed are uninvited. And can the uninvited open a home? If a guest can't, then certainly not the uninvited for the same reasons, only more so. This is easy enough when thinking about house guests, for instance. But what if we think through the example when it comes to homelands, to nations? For instance, because the US is a nation defined by its settler colonialism, can it be hospitable to refugees should it choose to do so? In other words, would this be hospitality in the true sense of the word, for wouldn't settlers be uninvited in the first place? Relatedly, would any nation that could properly be said to be able to host have the right to refuse refugees, something that would, in a sense, give them the power over life and death regarding non-citizens? These are clearly difficult questions, but perhaps part of the difficulty stems from conflating the notion of home with a space belonging to the one at home. Perhaps it's the case that home isn't a space, but a time.

Consider the question, Where are you from? We typically would answer this by naming a spatial place. But fromness doesn't always imply a space. For instance, I collect mid-century modern furniture, and I often remark that I have lamps from circa 1950. If lamps can be from a time, why can't people be from a time also? But why think in terms of time here? We might consider thinking about being from a time instead of being from a place inasmuch as being from a time allows us to share absolutely with regard to being-with.

In the most literal sense possible, space cannot be shared. If we map out space into coordinates, we can say that a certain object with extension occupies a space within coordinates x, y, and z. No other object with extension non-identical to the object occupying that set of coordinates can simultaneously occupy that named space. So, while space cannot literally be shared absolutely, time can be. As it relates to objects existing in the same time, this is what we call coexisting. When we coexist, we occupy spaces alongside each other while sharing the time of synchrony. If we orient our being-with as regards hospitality away from what can't be shared absolutely, orienting instead toward what can be, we avoid needing to make an ought to out of a literal impossibility. Space literally can't be shared—at least as far as Euclidean spaces go—and because ought implies can, we need to look elsewhere when thinking about what we ought to share. The only sharable, non-spatial quality of home is the time of home.

Is to think of home and coexistence in terms of time a move, let's say, to simply reduce settler guilt? No, this is a move to show a possible way forward regarding coexisting. Because we can't literally share space, in trying to share space in the way of existing alongside of, we need to draw boundaries of what space counts as shareable, and to those boundaries, we must assign invited occupants. This is the process of nation making on a large scale, of assigning property on a smaller scale. But this isn't without trouble. The political attempts to address this, but because the political gets caught up in the spatial, it can't literally solve—that is *completely*—a problem having no literal solution.

When orienting ourselves through shared time, we understand that we share time with all beings, including ontic beings such as the land. As such, because what exists within extended space lacks any stable identity over time, we need to have an ethics that's accommodating of time, especially of the kinds of time that are necessarily shared. And as such, we might turn to urgent ethical concerns such as, What shall we do in the Anthropocene? We can't fail to account for the time we share with the land. It's through such a perspective that we should understand being from.

Home Is Where the World Is if Being From Is Just

What does it mean to want to save the world? We sometimes get so caught up in our project of changing the world for the better that we don't first stop to think about what the world itself is. What is this world that we're wanting to preserve? On the one hand, the world is the place into which we continue to find ourselves being thrown. First, without prior consent, we're born into a particular set of circumstances, and as we continue our lives until the points of our death, the world rarely checks in with us regarding what we want. It's for this reason that a concern for justice becomes important. When the world into which we're thrown isn't conducive to our dwelling in it because it unfairly brings us suffering, we should reason that it's only rational that this unfairness be undone. And it's in this that we can come to blame the world, but though we may have now come to think of the world as being inhospitable, as being a place where we're unable to flourish, we still may not have begun to consider what the world is, exactly, for thinking of the world as only inhospitable would seem necessarily incomplete. Without a potential to be otherwise, why would we want to preserve something in which we ourselves can't be preserved?

Still, how is it, we might ask, that an unfair inhospitability can even belong to the world, belonging to it inasmuch as it's a fault of the world? It must be that our relation to the world can't only be one of thrownness, for if this were the only relation, then our relation to the world is that of a mere container. Containers *qua* containers can only contain. Just as a full water bottle only contains water as a brute matter of fact, containers don't contain either unfairly or fairly. At most, they can contain something that's unfair or fair. Further, if we're thinking all this in the context of being able to change the world for the better, we must think that we can master a quality of the world beyond its quality of containment, mastering it in such a way so that that part of the world can come to be under our manipulation. It isn't worth the effort of wanting to save the world if the world is but an unchangeable container. That we continue to want to save the world means that we accept that the world is inhospitable because it's now unfair, but by imagining and working toward something otherwise, the world can indeed become hospitable, allowing us to flourish through the well-planned guarantee of a fairness maximizing the minimum share of goods. Though we're thrown into it, the world has a manipulable quality, and to change the world, we need to get our hands dirty.

But is the world such that it's fully under our manipulation? In a very literal way, I can't manipulate something that I'm unable to put my hands on. I must have the ability to be in touch with something in order to manipulate it. I thus can't manipulate something like the weather because I can't touch the heavens. The sun and moon that cause the seasons and the changes of tide are beyond my reach, yet they're part of my world inasmuch as I live among them. Still, there are parts of the world that I can indeed manipulate. Thus, I can build shelter from a sun that gets too hot, and I can build this shelter away from where I anticipate the tides to rise. But building my home inland in a cooler climate is only a response to a particular type of inhospitability. These are choices I've made to manipulate the world in response to brute, unchangeable givens. Brute, unchangeable givens aren't themselves either unfair or fair. Heat and rising tides aren't in themselves an issue of justice. However, turning away climate refugees who seek to escape places where it's become unsafe to live … that definitely is. It's especially an issue of justice when we're at least somewhat responsible for having had a hand in making certain aspects of the world brute and unchangeable.

Still, here's yet another way to think about all this: If the world can be at fault for being unfair, worthy of praise when it's not, then we're giving over to the world a share of our agency. As a co-agent, the world can't *only* be a container. For we who orient ourselves to the world as beings among other beings like us, the world isn't only a container because the world is also comprised of what it contains. Just as a bottle of water is neither only the bottle nor only the water, but both, for us the world is both the container of beings and the totality of beings contained within it. And as we know, the world contains: 1. brute, unchangeable givens, 2. things that can come to be under our manipulation, and 3. the totality of beings just like ourselves. Can beings just like ourselves come to be under our manipulation? Sometimes yes, sometimes no, and the question of whether or not they should be manipulated when they can be … that's an issue of justice, too. Certainly, the world can become unfairly inhospitable because through manipulation, certain people have made it just that. And, at least in terms of the question with which we started, we'd like to save the world. If the world is at least partially made up of those who don't want to save us, then saving the world isn't an unfathomably large project because the world is unfathomably large. The world is large in this way indeed, but saving our oppressors and would-be oppressors is what makes our task epic.

So, is it too much to want to save the world given what the world is? Can we save something that contains those who don't wish to save us? When we think globally in terms of the political, this is a want that we can never fully realize as individuals. Though we may start with a fiery zeal that makes us naive enough to think we can do it all alone, that usually goes away by the end of the first few years of graduate school. Even as individuals wanting to save the world, we still enter into the project with a me-against-the-world mentality, for as an individual in this context, the other of myself is still the world. Again, the world is large, and those who have no interest in saving us are many. Me against the world is a battle that one can never win, a battle, we might note, that one shouldn't even need to fight. Though becoming no longer naive about how we might fare alone can plunge us into nihilism, nihilism is but another version of naivety. Ideally, we mature into the realization that we should indeed want to save the world, that it can be done because we never have to be alone so long as we have willing allies, and that we should therefore go about our epic task by starting to build community.

In wanting to build community, we might look to the political. After all, if we want to have justice, we need recourse to the political. Justice isn't possible without the political, for the political is necessary to ensure that the conditions of the world be hospitable for us, hospitable so that we might flourish in the world as human beings. At bottom, the political is our only recourse against oppressors who don't want to save us. However, the political always stops short of accomplishing our flourishing. The political can ensure that we have the means by which to flourish, yet it can't flourish for us. Thus, the political is in service of the hospitable, but if we're to dwell and flourish in the world, we need to start with the smallest unit. But what is this smallest unit?

The smallest unit of community is the home, and if we're to be flourishing human beings, our home must be as large as the world. Thus, the world is that which constitutes our home, and when we want to save the world, really, what we wish to do is to have the world be such that it's hospitable, hospitable so that all beings such as ourselves can call the world their home, and this because they're allowed to feel at home everywhere. To want to save the world is to want to save our home. To want to save the world is always a question of how to attain a particular state of hospitality, a state of hospitality opening the entirety of the world to everyone who now is and to everyone who shall later be. To want to save the world is to want to restore humanity to both: 1. those of us who are treated as though they're less than human and 2. those of us who are treated as though they're somehow more. And when it comes to human flourishing, to want to save the world is to engage in a project of absolute inclusivity, for everyone must be welcomed home. This isn't even to mention all the other sorts of living beings for and to whom we should feel responsible.

Not Always an Issue of Rights

For our purposes, let's define welcome as a hospitality that's freely given without obligation. Welcome isn't, then, by this definition an issue of justice. Welcome isn't an issue of justice because justice is obligatory. Justice is obligatory either through the letter of the law only, or through both the letter of the law and an ethical commitment. It's for this reason that we need a commitment to be as hospitable as we can be, because it can't be demanded of us. Put simply, that no one can force us to be nice people doesn't mean we needn't be, and we should be because no one can force us.

The seeking of justice, then isn't, and can't be, our right to feel at home everywhere, even when we've not been invited and are explicitly not welcome. There are at least some instances wherein we should take *no* to be a perfectly reasonable answer. It's in this sense that welcome is also an expression of love. We of course should be allowed to pick friends and romantic partners as we so choose, at least we should be from a rationally ethical perspective. Thus, we can make demands for justice, but one shouldn't make requests for love that are like political demands. We can't demand that others be hospitable. Hospitality needs to be given, and if it isn't, it can't be taken with any self-righteous entitlement. Thinking in this way is to partake in the same flawed logic of the settler colonizer. Just as I can't demand that you welcome me into your home, I can't assume that I should feel welcomed everywhere. Seeking justice isn't, and can't be, our right to feel at home everywhere, even when we've not been invited and are explicitly not welcome. Again, there are at least some instances wherein I should take *no* to be a perfectly reasonable answer. Let's pursue this through a thought experiment.

As a cisgender man, I wouldn't have been welcomed as a student at Scripps College. Is there any basis on which I can make the argument that this admission policy is unfairly exclusionary? For instance, if the position of admitting only women is to serve a community of people who would've otherwise been marginalized, can I make the argument that a certain intersection of oppressions I may have experienced because of identity are generally equivalent to the position of being marginalized as a woman? I'm a person of color; I have the invisible disability of epilepsy, for sure—and it's at least been suggested by psychiatric professionals that I'm not neurotypical in other ways—and I grew up in a low-income household. Would this make me more marginalized than a cisgender, white, neurotypical woman who came from a wealthy family? If this is a comparison that's relevant, then we'd need criteria by which to compare. However, there isn't a marginalization calculus for evaluating situations such as these because this is the wrong question to begin with. Regardless of whether or not I may rightly feel unfairly excluded, I'm not really in a position to force welcome when I know I'm not invited, for if I've had to force an invitation, then that's not really an invitation. Relatedly, in recent years, women's colleges have revised their policies to be welcoming to trans women and non-binary students. Obviously, it's progress when institutions are welcoming, but let's attempt to think through more difficult questions: Does a women's college have the right to refuse entry to trans women? Alternately, can a women's college refuse to graduate a student who transitions from female to male while enrolled?

    The point of thinking through such questions isn't to determine whether or not we can judge the college to be bigoted—I prefer that term here to *transphobic*, for as someone who thinks through a psychoanalytic framework, I think phobia isn't quite right—bigoted if they don't answer *no* to both questions. For me, I think the answer to a question of bigotry would depend upon whether or not the exclusionary practices come from a place of love or hate. Expressing love for people includable in a particular way of grouping doesn't mean *ipso facto* that one hates all other groupings of people. This is true just as expressing love for my family, let's say, doesn't mean that I hate everyone else. Excluding practices of outwardly projected hate pretending to be inward expressions of love—like white supremacists insisting that their practices are merely expressions of pride for their own race—if exclusionary practices are made from a position of love, then I would argue that these don't necessarily count as bigotry stemming from hatred. Thus, I'll opine that a women's college refusing entry to trans women might not *necessarily* be bigoted. Would this be the right decision to make? That's a more complicated question. One could make the argument that although not coming from a bigoted place, the exclusion could uphold bigotry nonetheless. From an ontological perspective, it could serve to feed into the notion that there's an ontological difference between women and trans women. At least in my view, the difference isn't an ontological one because the difference isn't one of *being*, but of whether or not *becoming* involved transitioning, for in our current psychic economy, most people are to some extent subject to a process of sexed becoming. At least that's what I get from a Lacanian framework, one theorizing how becoming sexed is always already an ascendency through the symbolic order for all speaking beings. If one is interested in this particular perspective, Patricia Gherovici has written an interesting book on the subject called *Transgender Psychoanalysis*. I'll also opine that a women's college refusing to graduate a student who transitions from female to male while enrolled is also complicated. With regard to the latter, on the one hand, such a refusal could be maintaining a procedural consistency with a policy to serve those identifying as a woman, but then on the other, the execution of the actual practice could be taken to impose a form of cisgender normativity. My point is that we can have strong feelings for arguments on either side, but to determine the most ethical solution isn't one that would necessarily imply that we must start from a place that tries to figure out whether or not the initial policy came from a place of hate. It's possible to have such an argument with the assumption that the initial policy is well-meaning, though perhaps not just. Still, the original questions I posed inquire into whether or not there's a *right* to refuse.

Do you have the right to refuse hospitality based on beliefs that are untrue and bad? What if there's controversy? There's a complicated way to think through this that involves the question of whether or not private property should exist, namely: If it is an issue that we can never justly refuse to be hospitable, then we have to rethink whether or not we ought to have private property. But perhaps the simpler solution is this: Can I force those who don't to love me? Framed this way, the answer is simple. I can't. With regard to compelling others, the most we can do is to compel everyone to live such that we all share a fair community. For instance, the Americans With Disabilities Act (ADA) isn't an issue of mere welcoming. It was something that began to address an injustice. Namely, if what had been legally designated as public spaces aren't accessible to persons with disabilities, then the implication would be that persons with disabilities aren't members of the public. This is, by definition, clearly an injustice. Still, if we can't reasonably say that we can force people to *love* other people, this means that love and justice aren't always compatible. Acceptance can be forced up until the point of non-oppression, but when it demands that we be loved, it goes too far. I think this is why we need to be careful with making accusations of bigotry. From a justice perspective, exclusion isn't a sufficient condition of bigotry, nor is non-love. All this being said, I wish profoundly that there would be more love in the world. Regrettably, we have to wait for other people to come around. In the meantime, we need to do what we can to teach it and encourage people to have love as much as possible. And to teach love as it relates to justice, we should have criteria for determining when there's a lack of love, and how love is lacking, exactly.

The Offensive, the Oppressive, and the Reckless

Taken in a certain way, absolute inclusivity as a political principle may seem paradoxical, for wouldn't an absolutely inclusive political practice even include ideas that would undermine it? But again, being cautious not to make too hasty a dismissal, this is to take the principle of absolute inclusivity in a certain way, in the way that understands absolute inclusivity to refer to something that partakes in no form of exclusion. So, rather than jumping to the conclusion that a political practice founded upon absolute inclusivity isn't a viable one, one that isn't viable because it would leave room for, say, white supremacist groups, we might think of absolute inclusivity as something resulting from the negation of a negation. In other words, instead of thinking about absolute inclusivity as that which includes everything, perhaps we should take an absolutely inclusive political practice as one that *excludes* all unfairly exclusionary practices. This, for instance, solves the problem of the white supremacist groups. Because their political practice is unfairly exclusionary—to say the least—we can exclude them in the name of absolute inclusivity. Still, the solution of thinking of absolute inclusivity as that which negates the unfairly exclusionary gives rise to another issue. While the issue isn't itself a problem, it is something that gives us a responsibility. Namely, radically inclusive political practice must responsibly decide on rejection twofold: it must decide on what it should reject, and to do this, it must decide whether or not what it might potentially be rejecting itself rejects unfairly. White supremacist groups are easy decisions, but what about when political questions arise that aren't so easy, questions such as, Shall we honor military personnel at a university ceremony if they've partaken in what some people believe to be an unjustifiable war? While the white supremacist groups don't occupy a gray area, other things do. How might we begin to decide on such things?

I'd like to suggest that we begin by thinking through the idea of what unfair exclusionary practice is, and in order to do this, we'll also need to be able to identify what it isn't, especially when we're presented with something that might bear a close resemblance. In that spirit, I'd like to offer three categories: 1. the offensive, 2. the oppressive, and 3. the reckless.

In the moments of my exposure to it, something that's *offensive* upsets my sensibilities or angers me, yet the expression or practice of the offensive thing falls short of placing me in a situation of physical or psychological suffering from which I can't have easily removed myself. In other words, if something's offensive, then I can reasonably limit my exposure to it. Something that's *oppressive* places me in a suffering situation, physical or psychological, from which I can't have easily removed myself, and by exchanging my suffering for another's physical or psychological enjoyment, oppression benefits my oppressor. The *reckless* shares the first part of the definition of the oppressive, only there can be no exchange of suffering for enjoyment, for the reckless act either immediately or with a delay makes everyone involved suffer. Lastly, as a point of clarification, we aren't, properly speaking, offended by the oppressive and reckless. Instead, we should more correctly say that we're opposed to them.

Regarding all of this as pertains to our rights, we have the right to be free from both oppression and recklessness. We also have the right to be bothered and angry. We don't, however, have the right to be free from being offended. This goes too far. Granted that people aren't just being offensive on purpose, this leaves no room for dialogue. Sometimes, we need to do the work of going beyond the emotions of having been offended to reach out to those whose ideas need changing. Further to this, even were one to not be willing to engage in dialogue, were it to be the case that all people practicing inclusivity have the right to be free from offense, then those among us who are the most easily offended would by that mere fact alone be the ones who rise to power, for they would have the most opportunity to silence others. This wouldn't be fair, for we should oppose our oppressors and the reckless, but we mustn't oppose either by becoming oppressive or reckless ourselves. Becoming oppressors is a possibility inasmuch as we might someday get our way when the current institutions of oppression and recklessness are torn down. When things are torn down, other things will come to replace them, so we mustn't replace them with the same thing, only with a different cast of characters.

And to push this all a bit further still, I certainly should never be offended by the mere existence of any person, for offense toward the mere being of another is nothing other than bigotry itself. Even if we're thinking about an oppressor, we should remember that though oppressors have qualities that belong to their mere being, we must not mistake any identity arising from those qualities of mere being for oppression itself. We should work against essentialism, for essentialism benefits none.

Regarding this last thing, I think we can elevate the general point—which is really nothing other than the time-honored progressive commitment to being non-essentialist—to the status of an axiom. Framed another way, in "Notes on Terrible Educations: Auto/Ethnography as Intervention to How We See Black" I think Dominique C. Hill and Durell M. Callier writing together as Hill L. Waters, their Black feminist love praxis project, put it best:

> "The first thing you do is to forget that I'm black. Second, you must never forget that I'm black," Black lesbian poet Pat Parker (2016) asserts as a productive pedagogical approach for White people who wish to befriend her (p. 76). In other words, see all of me but do not make particular parts of me, race for instance, the sum total of it all.
>
> *(542)*

Still, even with a commitment to non-essentialism, when attempting to speak across another type of difference, how might we comport ourselves when we confront the condition of reasonable and just disagreement?

When Philosophy Class was Over

Mostly, we discussed politics, religion, and all the other things that you wisely don't discuss with family during a holiday dinner. Did we get mad at each other from time to time? We did. We argued for what we argued because we were passionate about it, and that can of course get emotional. But for all that went on in the classroom, it was often the case that we'd go get lunch afterward, always the case that we were still friends enough to have been able to have gotten lunch, even if we actually didn't eat for this reason or that. That was in undergrad, and this very same dynamic continued throughout grad school when I took theory classes. If only we could've kept that dynamic when it was the case that I became faculty and had colleagues!

When we become professors, why can't we seem to remember that reasonable people can disagree and still remain friends? Why is it that we can mutually decide to never speak to each other again over a thing no more important than the other someone teaches a class too similar to ours, one wherein their methodological approach is slightly different? Do we feel that the stakes are so high, unreasonably so or not, that we get so stressed out that we forget to be decent to each other? Is it that any lived experience of academe necessarily takes place on the set of *No Exit* or some horrible Pinter play? In the case of the former, let me add some of my own punctuation: No! [Exit.] In the case of the latter, I'd rather not party like it's my birthday.

It's often the case that our work may be explicitly focused on building community, but then when it comes to our interactions with each other, we tear it down when we tear each other down in petty ways. At other times, we may have a research focus on better forms of governance, yet we can't be troubled to go to faculty senate meetings. I've met people who both keep Chantal Mouffe on their bookshelves and also set out to annihilate the careers of colleagues who think differently. Again, what part of being a professor makes us so horrible at working together?

Perhaps we're too focused on glory. When we're too focused on glory, our aim can shift away from its originally good target, the target of making the world better through the pursuit of knowledge and truth. When we're too focused on glory, we fight as one does in Hegel's account of master versus master. But the ultimate goal shouldn't be for the prestige of recognition. If our own egos are at stake, then it's no wonder that we can hate each other for tiny things. Maybe that's why when before we attained degrees recognizing our mastery, we had a better time of it. In a battle for recognition as the master, one has to subjugate. But that never works out for anyone. It's here where we should remember that absolute knowledge, at least according to Hegel, goes to those who've gotten out of this battle for recognition.

I know that those of us who want to be attendant to building community, especially academic discourse communities, sometimes make it sound as though we can never have heated disagreements with each other. Again, if we use the model of having lunch after philosophy class, this isn't the case. I myself am not afraid of heated debate. In fact, I think it's important to have it. The furnace doesn't have to be on full blast all the time, but sometimes it's the winter, and we're discontented.

Doing philosophy is boldly risking being radically mistaken. Sure, there are times when we can both be right, but when I'm asserting the negation of something particular, the negation of what you're arguing to be true, how can it be the case that one of us isn't wrong? If it's something important, let's not be afraid to argue. Let's not be so cowardly that we don't engage with anyone with whom we disagree. Also, let's not be so thin-skinned that we shut down any reasonable questioning of what we believe by asserting that those who dare engage us are some kind of bigot against our cause. Not to say that there aren't bigots, of course. We just can't *ad hominem* our way out of a good question from someone who isn't.

So, if we can give the benefit of the doubt to people who are our colleagues—at least the nice progressive ones—and take it as a foregone conclusion that we're all at least well-intentioned and for the most part on the same team, then shouldn't we be more open to each other? Shouldn't we be grateful that people take the time to argue with us because they care? Peace and love, yes. But being open to each other doesn't mean that we subscribe to some unattainable idea of community, one wherein everyone gets along at all times. If it were the goal to get along at all times, then we'd never utter anything more than flimsy platitudes disguised by the gravitas of academic jargon. What's the point of saying nothing at all just so that no one can say that you're wrong? That isn't what discourse communities are because that isn't even discourse. Again, it isn't a strong community if there's no ethic of love, but since when does love mean that we all find ourselves in agreement by default? We have to work toward consensus if that's what we're looking for. And sometimes consensus isn't even a thing we want. Above all, love is that which binds us together in spite of disagreement. And in love, there can be no singularly messianic and glorious me, for at the end of the day, it doesn't matter who's right, but what's right. If we stick to this principle, we'll all be friends, at least eventually.

Where Does Autoethnography Go?

Political being must account for both those with whom we find no shared political orientation and for non-rational actors. However, political being, strictly speaking, entails acting as though one is governed. When we're free to do otherwise, but agree to do only what's prescribed because it's efficacious regarding achieving a valued end, then we partake in political being. Political being follows prescriptive laws. We might, then, be led to believe that modes of being other than political being are for the most part free, with the exception being how beings are subject to physical laws. Physical laws, as opposed to the *prescriptive* laws of governance, are *descriptive*. It isn't as though objects need to choose to obey the laws of gravity, for instance. Beings such as objects can't but be subjected to gravity; they're unfree to be otherwise. We only ever observe objects behaving according to the laws of gravity because descriptive laws are by definition laws persisting outside of obedience or disobedience. Descriptive laws are outside of obedience or disobedience because they describe what is beyond what can be willed. But are beings really as free as all that? Outside of the prohibitions of prescriptive political laws and the confines of descriptive physical laws, are beings otherwise ungoverned?

Human beings who have free will are still governed by our position in the world. This means that choices are shaped by the time and space in which we find ourselves thrown. For instance, while I may choose to leave the place of my birth, my choices are always limited *to* going to a place *from* where I leave, *after* the time of having been there. And should I have chosen to stay, I stay in the place where I find initially myself, after the time I had been. All these choices would've been different should I have been born at another time in a different place. Thus, to be human and have a will that can value this or that is to be subject to eudaimonistic arrangement.

Eudaimonistic arrangement isn't a physical constraint such as gravity, the constant that's the speed of light in a vacuum, or the laws of motion. These all pertain to objects whenever and wherever they are, given any conceivable arrangement of beings in the world. These laws allow us to make predictions about times in the future regardless of place. There is no physical force that pertains to the eudaimonistic arrangements made with regard to the flourishing of all, however. This type of arrangement comes from a causal chain for which there's no predicting law. The causal chain is only a particular realization of potential.

The causal chain pushes back on us when we step into particular arrangements that aren't attendant and respectful of our position in the world. For instance, mastering nature by imposing our will upon it through a technology that wasn't attendant to the world as our home hasn't served us well. Continuing upon such a trajectory will efface us. And this is to only speak to how we've interacted with the more than human in the world. When we interact just as badly with the humans other than ourselves in the world, things become just as bad.

We aren't attendant to our arrangement when we take up too much time and too much space, when we do this to leave no time for others who more urgently need either more time, more space, or both. Attending to our own will is important, but it isn't any more important than attending to the will of anyone other. And it's precisely this that we must remember when attempting to justly speak across difference, and this of course goes for reading across difference as the case may be.

V.

Fifth, from Pelias's "A Story Located in 'Shoulds'":

> We should continue to ask what our research accomplishes. Fundamental questions should drive our concerns: What work does the story we are telling do? Whose interests are being served? Why tell this story now?

(610)

Why do we do what we do? Would we do the same work should the condition of doing that work entail the effacement of our signature? Or is it simply that we serve our own interests? We need to answer such questions when thinking through autoethnographic method as it pertains to justice, and when reading these works of justice, we might be wise to understand the *why* of what we do. And in the time of now, a time when humans have threatened all life on the planet, I wondered about what the point of doing anything that doesn't address that could be.

Publish and Perish

Why, as according to the psychoanalytic dictum, might it be that to signify a thing is to at the same time kill it? Let's approach this question from the other end. Think of immortality in a literal way: What's immortal is that which can't die. What sorts of things do we know to have no capacity to die? Other than things that had no life to begin with, the only things that we can observe with the quality of being unable to die are those things that are dead already. Thus, if there's some sort immortality to be achieved in the act of signification, then might we not say that to signify a thing is to kill it? True, maybe this is but an all too clever argument for not wanting to publish one's scholarship, but apart from the cleverness, there might be something useful in thinking publication along with the notion of death. Namely, if we wish to prioritize publishing about things higher in a hierarchy of importance rather than on things lower, wouldn't it be the case that before anything else, we should choose to publish on matters of life or death, so to speak?

Is Any Research Not About The End of the World Important?

Regarding the Anthropocene, I've been threatening to write a paper about how we might look to post-war writings for answers about our current situation. When philosophers were thinking about a bomb that could potentially wipe out all life as we know it, wasn't this very similar to what we're now contemplating when thinking about global warming? There are of course differences. The bomb is quicker, perhaps more preventable should rationality prevail. The planet becoming too hot doesn't happen instantaneously, and it might be more difficult for rationality to prevail because the relative slowness of climate change gives us space for disavowal, disavowal as we understand the concept psychoanalytically, that is. In other words, with regard to the climate, we may know very well that all this is happening, but we act as though we don't. So says Žižek in "Ecology". Namely:

> For example, precisely in the case of ecology, I know very well there will be global warming, that everything will explode, will be destroyed. But after

reading treatises on this, what do I do? I step out and I see not the things I see behind me now ... that's a nice sight for me, but I see nice sights, birds singing. Even if I know rationally that it is all in danger, I do not believe that it can be destroyed. That is the horror of visiting sites of catastrophes like Chernobyl. In a way we are not evolutionarily equipped, not wired, to be able to imagine something like that. It is, in a way, unimaginable.

(161)

In any case, thinkings about technology from this era might be useful. Heidegger might be a place to start. That's where Hans Jonas starts. He was a student of Heidegger, but like Levinas, distanced himself when Heidegger's Nazism became apparent. Jonas isn't exactly a household name these days, but his *The Imperative of Responsibility*, written during the Cold War, is prescient. In a way, it may be a precursor to what has become our more-than-human thinking. This is what he says in Chapter 5:

There is no need, however, to debate the relative claims of nature and man when it comes to the survival of either, for in the ultimate issue their causes converge from the human angle itself ... We can subsume both duties under the heading "responsibility toward man" without falling into a narrow anthropocentric view.

(137)

While Jonas might not reject anthropocentrism as strongly as what's currently in fashion, he does make a good point about ethics early on:

The *presence of man in the world* had been a first and unquestionable given, from which all idea of obligation in human conduct started out. Now it has itself become an *object* of obligation; the obligation namely to ensure the very premise of all obligation, that is, the *foothold* for a moral universe in the physical world—the existence of mere *candidates* for a moral order [emphasis original].

(10)

As far as we can tell, humans are the only beings on the planet contemplating ethics. The question of at least Western ethics, "What ought I do?" has always presumed the existence of future humans, but what if we can't comfortably make this presumption? If we can't, then it had better be the case that we make existence of future generations our ethical imperative. This is our responsibility at the most fundamental level. And as he'll later clarify, Jonas doesn't think that this restricts us to an overly narrow anthropocentric view. No one was really talking about the Anthropocene back then, but he's right that if we don't start getting things right, we might end up killing mostly everything out there. So, if you can go along with all this, then might we not reframe our original question? Given that we haven't yet solved the problem about the world ending, should we be publishing anything else?

Importance as Pertains to Urgency and Otherwise

In the hierarchy of importance, I'd say that nothing tops the world ending. I'd also say that the most important publications would be ones that don't just talk about the world ending, but somehow push us further along in our project to keep that from happening. But that's not necessarily to say that before we figure all this out, we shouldn't publish on anything else.

For the moment, let's put aside the world ending and think about the problem that each of us faces, the problem of our personal world ending, the problem of our own death. It's a foregone conclusion that I'll die. Yet throughout the day, I do several things to avoid my death: I look both ways when I cross the street; I try to eat healthy; I eventually choose not to hug the adorable bear … But why should I put so much effort into avoiding death if, in the end, I know that I'll fail? In other areas of my life, one might expect that guaranteed failure should be enough incentive for me to not try in the first place. Why should I waste the effort? Without needing to psychologize myself, we can at least say that when I attempt anything for which my failure is guaranteed, it must be the case that partaking in the attempt itself is what's of value to me, not my success. So, as for the problem of my own death, it must be the case that what's of value to me is to live by rejecting death.

And what does it mean to reject death? It isn't the case that I don't accept that I'll eventually die. Nor is it the case that I disavow my own death, that I know very well that I'll die, but I act as though I don't. Further, it isn't the case that I forget about it, for I almost immediately remember my mortality when I see the grizzly. Rather, a rejection of death is a choosing to live in the face of the inevitable. In other words, but more generally, there are times when I choose to will even when I know that the thing that'll eventually negate my volition is just around some corner. And wouldn't this be the case for the ending of the world that encompasses all our worlds? If the outcome of death is inevitable, how shall we live? And how shall we live through the act of publishing? How shall we read of these sorts of lives?

I'm not going to literally save the world from the global warming catastrophe by reading or writing anything about what I read. That's really in the hands of politicians and scientists, at this point. But to say that only the most urgent thing is the only thing of importance is mistaken also. Because I'm neither a politician nor a scientist, that doesn't mean that I should stop living. I can concern myself with other important things in the meantime, in this meantime while I wait to see what the politicians and scientists come up with. Sure, I try to recycle, but we're clearly past the point of that turning anything around in the way things need to be. That being said, I still think the eudaimonist project of the autoethnographic, while it might not turn around global warming, is still of great importance. In the end, autoethnography as a eudaimonist discourse helps us to think through justice as it pertains to the fair distribution of suffering.

Toward Understanding Autoethnography as a Eudaimonist Discourse

This is from Arthur P. Bochner's "Suffering Happiness: On Autoethnography's Ethical Calling":

> In my opinion, we do not need autoethnographies of happiness, because every meaningful autoethnography addresses the question of happiness. Of course, most of us socialized into the post-Enlightenment formulation of happiness don't see, experience, or relate to autoethnography this way. That's why we need a richer, deeper, fuller grasp of the connection between suffering and happiness. We know that suffering is an inevitable part of every life story and that autoethnography is a powerful and evocative means of bringing vivid and resonant frames of understanding to one's suffering and trauma. Unfortunately, the forms of telling and showing suffering and happiness have created the impression that they are oppositional or antithetical. My argument is that happiness is at stake in every narrative of suffering, and thus the question of the possibility of happiness in the presence of suffering is central to the whole project of autoethnography.
>
> *(226)*

Why might suffering and happiness not be oppositional? When things are set against each other in a relationship of opposition, we often interpret the relationship between the two things as being something like inverse proportionality. In other words, the more you have of one thing, the less you have of the other and vice versa. Think about the directions of left and right in relation to a line segment, for instance. The points nearer to the left are less and less near to the right, and the points nearer to the right are less and less near to the left. In the center of the line segment is a point equidistant from the leftmost and rightmost points. One could say that the center point is 50% left and 50% right.

There are relationships, however, that appear to have a midpoint, so to speak, that doesn't partake in either of the things at its most extreme ends. Suffering and happiness, I would suggest, exist in this type of relationship. To imagine this relationship, let's say we map the degrees of suffering and happiness onto a line segment, suffering to the left, happiness to the right. As we move further and further right from the most extreme point of suffering, suffering decreases, and as we move further and further left from the most extreme point of happiness, happiness decreases. In the middle of this line segment is a point which is neither suffering or happiness. There seems to exist such a neutral point. Sometimes we report that we feel neither this nor that: Meh, I could be better; I could be worse. In other words, the zero-point of both suffering and happiness overlap. What we see here, isn't a relationship that can be expressed by inverse proportionality. In an inversely proportional relationship, the zero-point of suffering should overlap with the most extreme point of happiness, and the zero-point of happiness should overlap with the most extreme point of suffering. If the overlap of the zero-points of both is in the middle, then less suffering moves in the direction of happiness, and less happiness moves in the direction of suffering, but who's to say that the less you suffer, the more happy you are, and the less happy you are, the more you suffer. For instance, I could've replaced *suffering* with *angered* or *worried* or *tired* or *morose*. These would've worked equally well on my line segment, but shall we say that suffering, angered, worried, tired, and morose are all the opposite of happy? It appears that if any two things are connected by a zero midpoint, then they might not actually be opposites. They aren't necessarily opposites because moving away from the most extreme point of one thing doesn't necessarily mean that you move closer to the other. For things to be oppositional in this way, the most extreme point of each thing must overlap with the zero-points of the other thing.

So, why do we often place suffering and happiness on an oppositional spectrum? Perhaps we make this mistake because suffering is such a state that the more we experience it, the less we're able to experience anything else, whether that be happiness or what have you. The more suffering I have, the less I can experience happiness, but also the less I can experience a general appreciation for things, wonder, outrage, or surprise. Perhaps happiness is overwhelming in the same way. The more happy I am, perhaps the less suffering can seem to me. In any case, this is all just to say that Bochner is absolutely right here, and it wasn't until I read that that I realized anything that I did in this section opening with my citation of him.

Was That a Pat or a Slap?

What's Lacan's point in the following passage from *Seminar III*?

> When you give a child a smack, well! it's understandable that he cries— without anybody's reflecting that it's not at all obligatory that he should cry. I remember a small boy who whenever he got a smack used to ask—Was that a pat or a slap? If he was told it was a slap he cried, that belonged to the conventions, to the rules of the moment, and if it was a pat he was delighted.
>
> (6)

If we examine being struck through a strictly phenomenological framework, we might expect only the response of crying. A smack hurts. But it could be the case that we can't stop at the phenomenological. The sense of the smack needs to first be interpreted in order to make a response. In both cases, a smack would feel a certain amount of pressure upon the skin—perhaps, from a careful guardian, only that of a moderately entertained hand clap—but in the context of communication, the person receiving the smack needs to think about the intentions of the person giving the smack, and after so doing, respond according to the conventions. In other words, the raw datum of experience only becomes datum of something once it's interpreted.

Suffering

Let's have a look at a passage from "Useless Suffering" by Emmanuel Levinas:

> The passivity of suffering is more profoundly passive than the receptivity of our senses, which is already the activity of welcome, and straight away becomes perception. In suffering sensibility is a vulnerability, more passive than receptivity; it is an ordeal more passive than experience. It is precisely an evil. It is not, to tell the truth, through passivity that evil is described, but through evil that suffering is understood. Suffering is a pure undergoing. It is not a matter of a passivity which would degrade man by striking a blow against his freedom. Pain would limit such freedom to the point of compromising self-consciousness, permitting man the identity of a thing only in the passivity of the submission. The evil which rends the humanity of the suffering person, overwhelms his humanity otherwise than non-freedom overwhelms it: violently and cruelly, more irremissibly than the negation which dominates or paralyzes the act in non-freedom.
>
> *(157)*

In relation to of the passivity of suffering, the default of our being open to regarding our senses is comparatively an *activity* of welcoming. A pure undergoing, suffering is a submission to which we must submit, and our ability to sense is what makes us vulnerable. What's interesting for me in this passage is the distinction between suffering and pain. Because he sets up his discussion of suffering at first through a phenomenological framework, Levinas seems to want to clarify here that he isn't speaking of mere physical pain. It would seem that the suffering of the senses would be just that—pain—for the sort of suffering repulsion given to the senses is precisely what pain is. We pull away our hand from a hot pot handle because the pain repels us, for example. Still, to then try to make a space for suffering as something going beyond mere pain may seem to indicate that starting from the framework of the phenomenological might not have been the best place to begin. In other words, pain only compromises self-consciousness, and does overwhelm one's humanity, but not in the way that suffering does so with violence and cruelty. So, why not assert first that suffering has a quality that goes beyond perception? Are violence and cruelty objects within phenomenal perception? Isn't it the case that something that isn't painful can be experienced which nonetheless causes suffering?

I think these are good questions, but they miss the spirit of the argument that Levinas is trying to make. And while the passage above from Lacan might seem incompatible at first, it isn't if we understand Levinas to be making the same argument only in reverse. In order for Levinas to make this argument, he has to have recourse to a temporally reversed phenomenality. In other words, it isn't that there's something that causes for us an object in perception, but that a particular object in perception retroactively valances the identification of an object cause of perception. In other words, the object cause of perception affecting or impressing upon perception in suffering must be something that's evil. Thus, violence and cruelty might not be objects within phenomenal perception inasmuch as there's no human sense perceiving violence or cruelty, but rather, the phenomenological experience of suffering makes the object cause of that experience something violent or cruel. Lacan's observation and Levinas's argument might seem incompatible, but only if one fails to realize that Lacan is on the interpretive side of a phenomenal experience, Levinas on the side of an intention for action belonging to an actor.

The Insistence of Evocative Autoethnography

Let's start by keeping a passage from Lacan's *Seminar XI* in mind:

> The real is beyond ... the return, the coming-back, the insistence of the signs ... Is it not remarkable that, at the origin of the analytic experience, the real should have presented itself in the form of that which is unassimilable in it—in the form of trauma, determining all that follows, and imposing on it an apparently accidental origin?
>
> (53–55)

It used to be that I would sleep through my alarms. I would dream, for instance, that I was on a submarine and we were under attack, or that I was trying to escape from a burning building, or that I was watching a film wherein someone's alarm clock was sounding. Chronologically, this doesn't seem to make sense, for how would I be able to anticipate the alarm sounding to have a dream that would let me sleep through when it sounded? It could be that my biological clock was so accurate that minutes before, my mind put me in a dream situation in anticipation of what would prove to be the blaring box next to my bed, one that's been the recipient of numerous and tired slaps. However, it's more likely the case that I heard the alarm first, and that my mind constructed a dream to explain it so that I could sleep, and this would happen for several minutes as the alarm continued to sound. After all, that could be the very point of dreaming: creating a narrative explanation of why one can stay sleeping!

It could be that our attempt to apply signs to trauma is what allows us to retroactively approach trauma as trauma, as such. We encounter trauma in the real, in that which resists both the signifier and signified. The trauma we encounter is something that can't be assimilated, and as such, our encounter with trauma is always already a missed encounter. Sure, we have repression at our disposal, but it's only the signifier that's ever repressed. Affect, for instance, isn't subject to repression. One can't really bottle up emotions, as some say. The traumatic itself, whatever it is, is by definition that which can't be spoken or thought. Perhaps things around the trauma can be spoken or thought, but *trauma* is the name we give to that which can't be. Should we try to narrate trauma, our narratives only ever encircle it. We can never get at the trauma itself. The traumatic is what can be understood as what can't be narrated. Thus, our narratives regarding the traumatic are things that reverse the temporality of the experience of traumatic. When we can't assimilate something through narrative, we know that what we've experienced is trauma.

So if, as Bochner says, "autoethnography is a powerful and evocative means of bringing vivid and resonant frames of understanding to one's suffering and trauma," then we might understand evocative autoethnography to be that which delimits the boundaries—in the literal sense of framing, as Bochner says—of trauma by circling it with narrative. Further, these narratives are evocative inasmuch as the affects surrounding trauma can't in the first place be repressed. The affects may be kept secret or held in suspension, but these affects come forth in the narratives should we allow ourselves to express them. And herein lies the power of these evocative autoethnographic narratives. Although we can never fully assimilate the trauma itself, these narratives come closest to approaching trauma, and in their close proximity to the trauma, the narratives show us the shape of trauma. And thus, autoethnography isn't an attempt to narrate trauma away, but to make perceptible what trauma is—this otherwise unassimilable thing—by refusing to cease its narrative. It's here where autoethnography finds its imperative to continue in an insistent way, in its refusal to stay silent about trauma, in its refusal to keep trauma a secret.

Further, within the power of the evocative autoethnographic narrative is to circle the traumatic in such a way that allows us to approach trauma as the accidental with regard to when the happenings of the world throw us into a situation wherein our agency is negated and we're forced to suffer. Evocative autoethnography reaches back into the past and allows us to encounter a real beyond our control, a real beyond what can be said or thought, and narrate our agency back by creating for us a way to understand what can't be understood as precisely that which is beyond reason. In other words, evocative autoethnography is an attempt to come to give meaning to suffering. And it's through this attempt to give meaning to suffering that evocative autoethnography reclaims humanity when the evil of suffering attempts to rend it away. If we understand Bochner's words to the letter, it's herein that we can see autoethnography as a eudaimonist discourse. And coming back around to Pelias's fifth suggestion, I think this is a good answer to the question regarding what our research accomplishes.

2
BEING-WITH, HOME, LOVE

Quantum Superposition and Being-With

In "'Throughness': A Story About Songwriting as Auto/Ethnography," David Carless writes:

> From my early childhood onward, whether formal education or informal teaching, wasn't it all about imposition? Why can't I remember a sense of partnership, of being asked to do something in such a way that I wanted to do it?
>
> *(229)*

This resonates deeply with me. At first the carrot, then the stick, then apparently even carrot sticks. Much of my own education, too, had seemed like an imposition, and when not overtly impositional, education was accomplished through what I'm sure educators liked to think of as *encouragement*, but an encouragement that left us little choice in light of our other young desires.

As a kid, we were encouraged to read through the promise of food. It was something called the Book-It! program. After reading so many books, one was given a certificate redeemable for one personal pan pizza. Also, at the time, I was a fan of a series of books called *Choose Your Own Adventure*. They were written in the second person, and every so often, at the bottom of the page, you'd be given a choice. For instance, you're hungry and come upon mushrooms in the woods. Do you eat them? If so, turn to page 16. If not, turn to page 20. On page 16, you find that the mushrooms are poison, and your adventure ends. On page 20, you decide to not to eat the mushrooms, and you find yourself greeted by a gnome. Do you talk to the gnome? And so on, and so on.

Gnome or not, I myself always opted to eat the pizza with the mushrooms. I read and ate voraciously. However, I never really got how the *Choose Your Own Adventure* series worked, so I read them all straight through. Maybe this was no inconsequential contribution to my postmodern sensibilities, or at least my openness to postmodern literature when I came upon it in college. Perhaps this also helped me understand the idea of quantum superposition when I read Barad for the first time. I don't know.

When we think of the postmodern, we think of it for its rejection of grand narratives. Why reject grand narratives? Let's take a look at an insight from Donna Henson's "Fragments and Fictions: An Autoethnography of Past and Possibility":

> It is all too easy to forget that our grand life stories are lived moment to moment, chapter and verse, with little thought or attention given to a narrative arc. And in the absence of the narrative arc, we might all be characters in search of a story—picking our own path, choosing our own adventure. If only.
>
> *(222)*

First, what's a narrative arc, exactly? We think of a narrative as the particular way a story is told. This is different from the story itself. Think of the narrative as a representation of a story, the story being something that's different from its representation. I think this careful distinction between narrative and story is part of Henson's insight. The narrative arc, then, would be the trajectory belonging to a narrative, particularly a trajectory that in its arcing begins on a particular plane, rises above and out of that plane, then eventually falls back. This arcing refers to how a narrative unfolds through the reading of the narrative. Of course, this could be complicated by the fact that a narrative may be told in a way that doesn't conform to the temporal linearity of the story. Thus, in this instance of a non-linear narrative, there are two unfoldings. First, there'd be the chronology of how things would've unfolded in the chronological sequence of time pertaining to the story. Second, there'd be the unfolding of our reading of a narrative from beginning to end. In other words, the narrative arc and the unfolding of a story don't need to match.

What this tells us is that a narrative arc can be a reordering of the story it describes. Our grand life story, then, is the story of our life as it unfolds over the stretching of our being from birth until death. This grand life story consists of the temporal entirety of one's life inasmuch as it's what's lived from moment to moment. In other words, there's no skipping over of moments, a skipping over moments that necessarily needs to occur in any narrative that isn't coterminous with the grand story of our life, whether that narrative be linear or non-linear. What we see then, in thinking through the notion of a narrative arc, is that narratives are always already a stitching together of fragments of the grand story of our life, a stitching that can only result in a fiction. No narrative can be a complete accounting of all the moments in the grand story of our life, so all narratives must leave something out. They subtract something, and in their subtraction, they create an arc out of the everything. Thus, there really can't be such a thing as a grand narrative. The grand narrative isn't a realizable possibility inasmuch as any realizable narrative needs to be incomplete. There are parts of our lives that necessarily resist narration. So, grand life stories are how one lives from moment to moment, but grand life narratives can't be told.

When thinking of our grand life story as the stretching of our being from birth until death, a narrative arc can only be created after the fact. As Henson suggests, it isn't as though we're characters in search of a story—choosing our own adventure, so to speak—in the absence of a narrative arc that can only come after our death. It's only after our death that the possibilities pertaining to us are revealed. It's only after our deaths that the paths we didn't take become cemented as possibilities as such. Really, from our own perspective, our lives as we live them can only be without a narrative arc. Our lives as we live them are a *Choose Your Own Adventure* story read straight through. When you live your life straight through, you're confronted with possibilities that aren't yet realized as possibilities, for in the yet to come, who's to say what will remain as possibilities when it's unknown which possibilities become exhausted of their potential through actualization? All that we have access to is an arcless story, one filled with what seem to be an infinite amount of things that might be possibilities. And isn't this also the complexity that also comes with the being-with of our being as we experience it? The first time I came into contact with Professor Ulmer—the person who would become my partner, Jasmine—I literally ran away because I thought she was going to ask me about the article sitting too long in the production queue of a journal for which I was the managing editor. Several articles and years later, when I ended up running back, I realized that assumption was mistaken.

You choose not to talk to the gnome, but then at one point, you also choose to start a conversation. You sometimes eat pizza together, even though the casein in the cheese messes with her a bit. One time at Pizza Hut, you both recall the *Choose Your Own Adventure* stories. You continue not following the directions at the bottom of the page because there aren't any directions, let alone pages.

The World Time of Method

Let's examine an insight from Christina Ceisel's *Globalized Nostalgia: Tourism, Heritage, and the Politics of Place*:

> Itineraries are schedules of destinations, a rudimentary means of planning one's path. How do we develop our itineraries? What influences where we head? What inspires us to choose the routes that we take? Reflecting on my

itineraries and the expectations that have structured and informed my choices, I realize that my travels and experiences outside of "home" have been (unwittingly) routed through heritage—both personal and cultural.

(28)

If the way of method is a being along with on a path, then the stopping points along the way are destinations where particular truths are disclosed. Here, Ceisel makes the case that itineraries are plans regarding a path, plans that include schedules of destinations. If in some sense ethnographic methods themselves involve travel to what's outside of where one feels at home, then the consideration of itineraries as applied to ethnography would add the dimension of time. As a method with an itinerary, rather than simply being a path one travels along with others, there are scheduled destinations. But what sort of time is marked out on this schedule?

The time of itineraries as applied to ethnographic method aren't the same as the itineraries of, say, a vacation. There's not a necessary departure time wherein one needs to catch a train, for instance. Rather, to include itinerary in method would only be to include world time. In other words, arriving at the destination of a truth is a particular time around which we orient ourselves as beings. Here, I plan to arrive at a particular truth, and once I arrive, that's the time of a disclosure. But because I have an itinerary, I orient myself such that I might arrive; I orient , myself around the time of arrival such that it becomes exactly that. But let's be more clear about world time and how it differs from the time on a clock.

The time of methodological arrival, the time of coming upon a disclosure of truth, is the same, let's say, as a bedtime. Because I wish to sleep, I orient my being around the time when I'll fall asleep such that I might get there. Again, this isn't necessarily to have a particular bedtime in mind, one involving particularly positioned hands on a clock, but only a will to fall asleep for which I make room as I orient my being towards it. Such are world times.

So, world time is the time of method, and Ceisel's method isn't one that's only ethnographic, but because the itineraries of this method are routed through both a personal and cultural heritage, what we see is that Ceisel's method is autoethnographic, and because we arrived at this conclusion regarding Ceisel's work, we could make the case that a component of autoethnographic methods might be the itinerary. Autoethnographic methods take up itineraries that put the autoethnographer in a time during which they're away from home. And isn't this time being away from home sometimes experienced as being productively lost, being lost as Benjaminian *flâneur*?

Lost in Readings and the Four Forces of Truth in Autoethnography

About being at a young age and finding his way back from having become lost in the woods, Christopher Poulos writes this in *Accidental Ethnography*:

Eventually, I emerged from the woods about a half-mile down the road from where I started and I thought, "Huh. I should try that again" ... Since that day, I've had this fascination with the idea of being lost, and of finding my way back to where I started—or to a fresh, new place. There is something about getting lost, and then getting "un-lost," that changes you.

(52)

What is it about getting lost, and then unlost that changes you? This lostness is a productive being lost inasmuch as it produces a change, but why? I think such a productive lostness might be related to the forces of truth that we find in autoethnography, and I believe that there are at least four: 1. disclosure, 2. epiphany, 3. affective evocation, and 4. the performative. When something has yet to be disclosed, it's in a sense lost to those for whom what isn't spoken is kept as a secret, the not revealed. And if an epiphany is what comes before a revealing of truth, then the truth had always been there, but was momentarily lost as it awaited being discovered. Once the truth is brought back into the open—and we come upon a clearing in the woods, one might say—we can 1. let the truth itself speak by calling out to it through the affectively evocative, and 2. know that the way has been cleared such that the truth can speak in repetitions through the form of the performative. When the truth itself speaks, it's from this that we determine value, and thus the affectively evocative and the performative can become evaluative with regard to these values. If we can take Poulos's passage as a metaphor for autoethnography as a philosophical practice—and the seeking of truth in general—then getting lost and unlost is roughly the tension that the philosophy of autoethnography narrates for the reader. Autoethnography narrates at least two kinds of revealing, which correspond to becoming lost, at least two types of letting the truth itself speak through the affectively evocative and the performative, and these correspond to becoming unlost.

Again, both disclosure and epiphany are types of revealing, but they're also revealings respective to two different kinds of closure. Autoethnographic disclosure dis-closes; it reveals an open that had been closed off by an economy of silence or an economy of shame. Similarly, autoethnographic epiphany realizes what had been there all along, but was closed off from realization because it was hidden by ideology. This puts disclosure within the realm of the *oikos*—the home—and epiphany within the realm of the *polis*—the political. Because autoethnographies can be both disclosive and epiphanic, autoethnography has the ability to address humans both as those who are at home in the world and as those who are political subjects.

Both the home and the political have rules pertaining to fairness, but rules of a different kind. The rules of the home are rules pertaining to a putting into order, rules that take the form of directives. The rules of the political are the rules of a governing constitution and of ideology, rules that take the form of prohibitions. Because it isn't merely personal, autoethnographic disclosure isn't what Foucault would've called confessional. Autoethnographic disclosure is accountable to matters of being-with as it pertains to feeling at home. Being accountable to these matters moves us beyond political justice, something only having recourse to prohibiting laws. And because the home functions through directives that put into order, rather than merely being left to craft responses to what we disvalue, autoethnography allows us to better understand fairness epiphanically by focusing on what we positively value. Once revealing has come to pass—once one has become unlost, so to speak—the truth can itself speak when it's called out to through the affective and can repeat itself through the performative. This is the meaning that autoethnography brings to a being at home, and if it's a eudaimonist discourse, to opening up the possibility of being at home at all times. Becoming lost and unlost, then, narrates the philosophical itself as an urge to be at home at all times.

Lastly, with regard to the at all times of being at home—all times comprising the experience of the past in present memory—autoethnography may be nostalgic insofar as it addresses the pain of returning home when one had been away, the literal meaning of *nóst-algia*. Nostalgia can be a sort of homesickness, and philosophy is in some sense this, too.

Homesickness

Quoting Novalis, Heidegger writes: "Philosophy is really homesickness, an urge to be at home everywhere." Heidegger points out that if there's an urge, or drive, to be at home everywhere, then we who philosophize aren't everywhere at home. And yet, what does that mean, to be driven to be everywhere at home? It doesn't mean to be driven to be at home merely here or there or every place in which we may find ourselves. No, this is to miss the implicit temporal dimension. "Rather, to be at home everywhere means to be at once and at all times within the whole" (5). And being within this whole, we find out, is being in the world. This is good, but might we offer another interpretation with regard to homesickness should this be our concern?

As the grammar has it, the urge to be at home everywhere is what homesickness is, and homesickness is also philosophy. Thus, it stands to reason—just as Heidegger has it—that philosophy is the drive to be at home everywhere. But can we really make these substitutions the other way around? While it may make sense to say that philosophy is the drive to be in the world, does it conversely make sense to define homesickness as philosophy? In other words, when one finds oneself in the state of homesickness, is one thus philosophizing? I doubt that Heidegger would have it that a child on an airplane who screams impatiently and incessantly, screaming having been told that home is still six hours away, is also partaking in philosophy. No, it makes sense that philosophy shares the driven quality of homesickness, but that homesickness doesn't necessarily share qualities other than that drive with philosophy. Thus, though we may say that to philosophize is to be homesick, we won't say to be homesick is to philosophize. Rather, we'll only say that to be homesick is to be driven to be at home everywhere. But does this make sense?

Following Heidegger's initial move, we too should note that one who has the drive to be at home everywhere isn't at home. By definition, being homesick implies that I am not at home. Now let's see where this takes us. If I'm not at home and have the drive to be at home everywhere, then the satisfaction of my drive would entail that I be at home in the place that is not my home. This could mean that being homesick is the drive to turn every space I occupy into my home to avoid homesickness, but this is more parsimoniously done by going to my home. In fact, that's how we would generally understand homesickness. But the fragment has it that the drive is not directed toward one's home, but everywhere. Novalis doesn't assert that to be homesick is to have the drive to return to the space of one's home.

One could at this point think that Novalis gives us a very poor gloss of homesickness. While we may be ready to dismiss this as nonsense or at least something overly complicated, we might instead squeeze from this seemingly odd formulation a powerful insight.

Is the everywhere in this formulation a mere place? If Heidegger, to serve his purposes, had to add a missing temporal determination to it—the at once and at all times—might we not think of everywhere as most saliently this temporal determination? Further, if home is included within everywhere, and everywhere is here most saliently a time, then would we not say that home is also essentially a time? Thus, we should formulate as follows: When one is homesick, one is driven to be at once and at all times during the time of home.

This doesn't involve such a convoluted satisfaction of the drive. The temporal duration during which I'm not at home is a time when I'm driven to be during the time of home at once and at all times. I'm not in this temporality at this point, so I experience this drive. Further, it's possible to be at home at once and at all times if it's merely the time that matters. We don't need to transform spaces. Thus, homesickness isn't a drive to be in the home. Rather, to be at home should be taken to be the state during which one doesn't feel homesick. One is at home when one feels at home. This is very different to say one is at home on the condition that one is in one's home. It's here that a passage from Devika Chawla's *Home, Uprooted* is interesting: "In some ways it seems logical: a break from home leaves him adrift, and thereafter there is no continuity in his life, just movement and motion" (104).

What of the movement and motion that anyone broken away from their home might feel, this feeling of being adrift? Typically, we think of movement and motion as a type of continuity. Movement and motion involve both space and time, and while space can be divided, we understand time as a flow. This is how one can get around Zeno's paradox of motion, it's in fact how Bergson solves the problem: to remember that time isn't divisible. But this is the time of the clock. The time of the world does admit of divisions. Now is breakfast time, work time, lunch time, work time again, home time. If we have a break from the time of home, then what typically is experienced as a continuity would set us adrift. We'd only have movement and motion as experienced through the time of the clock. We wouldn't have movement and motion as experienced as through the time of the world wherein we feel at all times at home. This would be a break, a crisis of home, and we'd be pained to return to the time of home should it ever happen that we are forced to spend time away from it. And further still, might it not sometimes be the case that we may be homesick with regard to that which becomes forever foreclosed to us as a possibility, something that becomes no longer possible through something other than actualization?

The Eternal Impossibility of Certain Returns

In "The Way We Weren't: False Nostalgia and Imagined Love," Anne Harris writes:

> When I was eighteen, I was legally allowed to petition for my birthmother's information from the State of New York. I called all the relevant agencies and asked outright for my birth information. I was told that apart from "non-identifying information" (like my mother's age and parents' cultural backgrounds), it was not my information to have, it was private information, and it was sealed. The intense powerlessness I felt marks the end of me believing that laws and rules had any moral or ethical traction.
>
> *(781–82)*

Here, I think we see an example of how the laws pertaining to the political might not be grounded in what's ethical, at least with regard to what's ethical regarding how we think of things pertaining to the home and the people we might want to feel at home with. Further, there's a truth that could be disclosed, a truth that's sought, but one for which disclosure is refused through remaining untold. Later in the article, writing about a documentary film she was making in her early twenties, Harris writes that she asked her parents several questions, including if they had any regrets. Her father told her this story:

> When they were in Mort Schulman's office to countersign the adoption papers, Mort made it clear to them that my birthmother's name was on the paper as well, although it was under a sheet of paper lying on top of the legal one. He told them her name was there, and he looked them in the eyes, according to my father, and said that he was going to leave the room for a few minutes and they could do what they wanted, and that if they looked at her name or moved that paper, he would never know and it was not the same as him disclosing her name, which was prohibited by law. He left the

room. According to my father, he said to my mother, "should we look at her name? Maybe we should write it down for later" and my mother said, "No. I don't want to know."

They signed the bottom of the form and waited for Mort to come back in and he withdrew the papers and they never had another chance to know her identity. He said that now, seeing the pain it had caused me, it was his only regret. But what is regret? A trace, a memory, a story untold? For my mother, it was a fiction that had severed its relationship to the possible in that moment.

(782)

Harris writes of the pain of an impossible return, the pain of never being able to know. She also tells us a story wherein there's a refusal of knowing what can be known, something that we can think of as a disavowal. In other words, the decision to not know what could've been known becomes a regret, for the disavowal is "a fiction that had severed its relationship to the possible in that moment," a fiction that severed its relationship to the possibility of disclosure.

It can sometimes be the case that some returns are foreclosed to us because the truth to which we may want to return had been kept as a secret. I think Harris's autoethnographic piece is exemplary inasmuch as it foregrounds the pain that can accompany the closure of truth such that the knowledge of truth can no longer be a possibility. Return could have been possible at a certain time, but once that time has passed, the truth can't be disclosed, instead remaining closed forever.

Autoethnographies often take up a foreclosure of disclosure. A general problem addressed in autoethnography, then, becomes how one can reclaim from the past such intense feelings of powerlessness, such feelings of which Harris writes. To put it in somewhat Nietzschean terms with regard to his problem of the eternal return, how do we say, "Thus I willed it," to a traumatic past that's beyond our own volition? This is a question we often find posed in autoethnography.

Reclaiming the Past Through Citation

Let's look at something from Norman Denzin's "Indians in the Park":

> Beginning with the sting of childhood memory, I follow Benjamin's advice concerning history—that is, to write history means to quote history, and to quote history means to rip the historical object out of its context. In so doing I create the conditions for invention, for discovery, for new ways of representing, and hence experiencing the past. The past flits by, like an image on the screen. To represent the past this way does not mean to recognize it "the way it really was." It means to seize hold of a memory as it flashes up at a moment of danger, to see and rediscover the past not as a succession of events, but as a series of scenes, inventions, emotions, images and stories.
>
> *(10)*

In this prefatory remark, we see from the outset that Denzin wishes to create the conditions for *invention*, to create the conditions for a finding out. To create the conditions for invention isn't itself to invent. To make claims to invention itself is to take ownership of exhausting a potential through the invention of the invented. To exhaust a potential is to partake in a type of closure. To create the conditions for invention, however, is to instead create paths leading toward a finding out. Such paths are paths that become the openings of ways. To open a way in this manner is to partake in the creation of method. To create method isn't to ordain an orthodoxy, to maintain that this or that opinion is the correct way, but to allow others to find their own way along the path. To create such an opening is to also create the conditions for what we might call *discovery*. And why create the conditions for discovery?

If to dis-cover is to open what had been closed, this is roughly what it means to dis-close. And to disclose in this way is what's contained in the term *aletheia*. *Aletheia* is truth as disclosure, as an opening again of the closed. To disclose through the use of language is to present the truth again, to make the truth itself speak. In other words, as Denzin says, it's to *re*present: specifically, "to represent the past this way does not mean to recognize it 'the way it really was.'" But why is this so? The truth of the past can only be experienced as memory. The time of memory isn't the chronological time of the clock, but the times of a particular when by which we orient our being, the times of the world as they pertain to the person who remembers, these times being framed by the stuff of memory itself: "scenes, inventions, emotions, images and stories." If the truth had remained closed to us in the past, then the truth of such a memory can't be a way that really was. And this is why there can be "the sting of childhood memory," the pain of returning, the pain that's nostalgia. Here, nostalgia is citational. It's a promise to have read a history, but to have read it from the perspective of the remembering of memory. When we move from nostalgia to a remembering seeking to reorient our being by the time of epiphany, then we're putting into dialogue: 1. the closed truth of the remembered past with 2. the disclosed truth of the now of having discovered. To rip the historical object out of its context is to reclaim the truth into the opened.

I understand Denzin's later work on the American West to have as its primary aim to be precisely this. Denzin puts the closure of truth accomplished by western epistemology into dialogue with perspectives informed by Indigenous epistemologies that had not been closed to truth in the first place. As per above, Denzin's inspiration comes from a reading of Walter Benjamin, but also, as one can see from how he frames his own project, there are hints of a philosophical framework informed by phenomenology, at least in the successive terms suggesting *aletheia*: invention, discovery, and representing. We might note that Denzin's earlier work, work such as his writings on emotion, do indeed take an explicitly phenomenological approach. And although this earlier work is perhaps more influenced by phenomenologists such as Merleau-Ponty, phenomenology is itself a tradition that includes a thinker of *aletheia* like Heidegger. If Heidegger himself represents a sort of end of history with regard to Western philosophy—in other words, if Heidegger's thought is the furthest that Western philosophy can go without changing its fundamental assumptions—then there's reason to challenge Western philosophy. Heidegger's affiliation with Nazism makes it clear that we need to discover and rethink what it was in this trajectory of thought that allowed Nazism to be compatible. It's for this reason that I've had a longstanding interest in thinkers who've tried to accomplish such a discovery and rethinking. Denzin, for instance—as he was recently quoted in a special issue in *Qualitative Inquiry* regarding the multiform uses of theory—has been known to say that theory is dead. Given what we've seen above, perhaps he believes that theory is dead because it's rooted in Western philosophy, a philosophy that not only gets stuck, but erases what could've gotten it unstuck.

Again, I see Denzin's later work as addressing the erasure of Indigenous epistemologies by Western epistemology, an erasure accomplishing a form of closure. For me, this is exemplified well in Denzin's text "Mother, Shane, and Sonny." We should make note of a subtlety not explicitly written in the text: The film *Shane* itself, a film taking place in the time of the settler colonization of what we've come to call the American West, depicts only the settlers. Perhaps it's commendable that the film lacks on-screen racist depictions that would've been commonplace for the time of production, but it lacks these depictions by erasing Indigenous peoples altogether. Denzin's late work seeks to address such an erasure, particularly as regards ways of knowing the world through what gets remembered. If erasure makes invisible what would've otherwise been seen, it's in this sense that I think his work is respectful. A paying of respect is a seeing again that's also a reflective looking back.

Respectable Humans

We compete when wanting access to a limited resource, one that others might also wish to enjoy. When resources aren't limited and all may enjoy, then there's really no reason to compete. In fact, it may be that we aren't even able to compete should a given resource be of a particular type. Being both non-rival and non-excludable, such is the public good, for instance. We can't use up all the lighthouse light, and you really can't stop anyone from using that light short of blindfolding them.

So, can we say that competition results from wanting to enjoy something that's limited? This seems to be the case for resources, but what of limited things in general, things not included under the category of resources? For aren't there things for which we compete that aren't resources at all?

Take playing a game, for example. If a game can be lost or won, then that game has competition, but the winning of a game wherein winning is a possibility isn't a resource. Still, the winning of a game is limited were the outcome of that game to produce at least one loser. The winning is limited by the rules of the game, the winner being stipulated by a particular outcome proceeding from the realization of the rules of play. If there must be at least one loser, the positions of winner aren't available to all. Straightforward enough, but what does such a line of thought have to do with respect? It has to do with whether or not we must compete for it.

Is respect limited? We often compete for it as though it were. Regarding achieving respect, when we try to outdo another—or perhaps even all others—we act as though respect can't be achieved by all. I may win your respect because your respect can be lost inasmuch as it can be taken away or never given in the first place. But this isn't necessarily to say that it's impossible for someone to have respect for everyone with whom one comes into contact. Though a particular person may never gain your respect, this isn't to say that your respect is available in only limited amounts. And true, the realization of respecting everyone might not be accomplished in practice, but this isn't so as a matter of inability. So, in this sense, it seems as though respect isn't limited, at least as regards the possibility of giving respect. Regarding giving respect, respect would only be limited were that respect to be submitted to a hierarchy: This person is the most respected, this other person respected, but less than the most, and so on. And were respect to be submittable to a hierarchy, then this would be to say that respect—at least certain kinds of it—admits of degrees, that one can respect more or respect less.

So, the giving of respect isn't limited by inability, but were the type of respect given to admit of degrees, would this mean that the position of being the most respected is limited? Yes, but only if the position of most respected be stipulated to be occupiable only by one. In other words, there would need to be the stipulation that there couldn't be ties for this position, that the most in this instance doesn't mean merely having attained a certain level of maximal achievement, but means instead that one is necessarily above all others. Oddly, such an achievement of being above all others doesn't necessarily entail that one's achievement be maximal. In any case, all this is to say that certain types of respect can be limited, but that they're limited doesn't mean that they couldn't have been otherwise. In fact, it's often only after a certain amount of work that we're able to make the limits. We at least need to take the time to make definitions and have rule making. And the last point is to say that when we compete against each other as colleagues competing for respect, we've somewhere stipulated in the system of our community that respect *should* be limited. And were we to vie for the position of most respected scholar, we see that we've at least tacitly submitted to a particular type of imposed limitation. Could it be the case that an unthought-through compulsion to compete is itself what causes us to impose artificial limits, at least in certain situations?

There are, of course, other types of respect that aren't hierarchical because they don't admit of degrees. To respect another as a human being isn't limited in this way, and if we relate to each other on this level, there's no need for competition.

The Seeing Regarding Respect and Perspective

Let's have a look at a passage from Art Bochner's *Coming to Narrative*:

> Don't get me wrong. I understand the desire to win the respect of your colleagues and peers. People like you and me were students for so many years that we lost perspective. We've always wanted to please our teachers and mentors. Then we had to win the approval of our colleagues and senior professors who would judge the significance of our work. Rarely have we been asked who would use our research, though that's the really important question. What difference are we making in the world out there?
>
> *(265)*

Respect involves the gaze inasmuch as it's literally that which is a looking back. When we're seen, we're never seen from the place from which we see. The eye that sees can see many things, but never itself. And thus, the glory of respect comes from a place that we must imagine, for we can never experience it for ourselves. Respect belongs to the specular other, to the other of the imaginary. And here, we speak of the imaginary not as that which is of the imagination, but the imaginary that's the result of the duality of specularity, the result of the duality of the image. We must imagine respect for respect can only be when we have a counterpart in the dual relation of the gaze. To have respect is to have won the looking back of an other. Further, when we see, we always see through until our seeing beyond is obstructed by an object, by the object consisting of what we see. It's for this reason why the specular, why the imaginary, describes a dual relation. There's no mediating element, for when we see, it's only the one who sees and the object seen without a mediating between. To see an object, the between before that object must be invisible to the seer. This seeing through is what we literally mean when we speak of perspective.

So, how might one lose perspective, especially regarding respect? To lose perspective regarding respect would mean that something occludes our seeing through. To have lost perspective here means that something comes between us and our specular other. But what can such a thing be? Could such a thing be desire itself? When there's desire, something comes between us and the object. Desire itself, of course, has no object. At most, it has an object cause. When there's desire, what comes in between is the subject, and it's the subject that renders into signifiers what would've otherwise been the two in a specular, imaginary relation. As Lacan says time and again, "The signifier signifies a subject for another signifier." In other words, introducing an intermediating third, desire renders what would've otherwise been an us into signifiers and makes us part of what we call the symbolic. To desire, then, is in this way to lose perspective with regard to respect. This is what happens when we have the question of, "Who am I for the Other's desire?" Isn't this the very question of whether or not we're regarded with respect, of whether or not we've come to please? We don't know how we might be respected inasmuch as the originary relationship involving a non-occluded other has now something in between. Like not seeing the forest because it's obstructed by all the trees, desire's introduction of the subject occludes our perspective to the other. The subject is what's in the way because it's what mediates in the relationship of desire.

Serving the pleasure of our teachers and mentors, and then at the pleasure of our colleagues and senior professors, turns us, as we've said, into signifiers. And inasmuch as we find ourselves alienated in our work, we're held accountable to not only our work's significance, but we're held accountable to the very significance of ourselves. We're signifiers inasmuch as the who of who we are is that which is accountable to our significance. But as the passage concludes, this is the full account of how perspective is lost in this particular context: It shouldn't be a question of our personal significance as scholars. It shouldn't be a question of the respect we desire to win. The question should be about the difference we make in the world. Our research is important when it makes a positive difference, and this has little to do with what we ourselves come to signify. And if this is good to remember regarding the respectability of our work, the work that allows we humans to flourish in the context of other humans, isn't this good to remember regarding being-with in general, especially with regard to those with whom we're at home, or at least those with whom we'll eventually be at home? It isn't incidental that this passage comes in a subsection of the same book titled "The Meeting." The chapter opens with a bit of dialogue followed by:

> You may wonder what I'm doing here. Well, we didn't arrange a date, if that's what you're thinking. Instead, we called a "meeting." Presumably, we are getting together to discuss ways of connecting the graduate programs in sociology—Carolyn's department—and communication, my department. But academic meetings between two people rarely take place in such a beguiling setting— soft music in the background, wine and cheese on the table in front of us, dogs on our laps.
>
> (251)

Recounting the past, Bochner is in Ellis's living room.

A Song for You?

Regarding those to whom we'd like to feel at home in terms of romantic relationships, why is it that love songs never get it quite right? We'd like to share meaning and time with such people, but sometimes love songs get it absolutely wrong. For instance, in his introduction to a special issue on song, "'A Song for You'/'Killing Me Softly': Lyrical Dialectics of Design, Desire, and Disdain (A Performative Introduction)," Bryant Keith Alexander writes:

Growing up my sister's albums were mostly of Black men singing presumably to Black women, or by Black women singing presumably of the Black men they desired (or who broke their hearts). And I would watch my sister moaning along and grooving along with those songs imagining that HE was singing to HER, or SHE to HIM—the object of her desire. And as her gay younger brother, I too would moan along and groove along, imagining that those men were singing to ME, and I to THEM—the object of my desire. But I knew they were not singing to me because these male singers often sang of intimacies of particular physiologies that negated my child-like imagination to intuit my possibility. And I wondered who would sing songs like that to me—songs with such ache and desperate yearning, to me, a Black gay boy living in the south.

(771)

Here, the context of heteronormativity makes the songs not quite right, and we see that full identification is foreclosed when it comes down to descriptions of the implied addressee. But I think the profundity of Alexander's insight here is one speaking to the fragility of how objects of desire get constructed to be objects of desire in the first place. We get this in the juxtapositioning of desires. Typically, if we want a love song on an album to be sung to us, what we don't want is for the fantasy to be broken. What fantasy? That the text of any song on a popular album is written such that it can be read, so to speak, by an implied reader who can be nearly anyone. The gender pronouns do put a restriction on this anyone, but they'd fit any relation of *to her* or *to him*, as the case may be.

There's a particularly brilliant love song that goes something to the tune of the singers—it's a group—asserting that they don't care who you are, or where you're from, or what you had done in the past, so long as it's for them that you have love. There aren't any restrictive gender pronouns. So long as the listener might love this band, it's all good. Is this an exemplar of a truly progressive love song? Sure, young people may swoon—the band members are attractive—but would anyone really want this kind of love when taken absolutely literally? Question: For what reasons do you love me? Answer: It doesn't matter, really, because as I asserted repeatedly, I don't care! So, even were I to be a convict who just came from a prison after serving a sentence of financial fraud, and I may have helped steal an election, thereby weakening democracy for a long time at the very least, that would be just fine. That you don't seem to have any standards doesn't make me feel all that special. At bottom, there's something that really shouldn't sit well with us regarding the sister's desire as described by Alexander. It's only a comfortable identification on her part inasmuch as it's purchased at the cost of a disavowal.

There's an extent to which generic love might be a description of unconditional love. If we want unconditional love, then such a boy-band lover should be ideal. But this is where the fantasy of being an object of desire is particularly fragile. If you don't care about any of my qualities—you love me on no condition pertaining to them—then I can't really feel worthy as an object of love. I can't feel respected, because you didn't even look. It's indeed a sad fact that there are certain configurations of desire for whom the fantasy of this sort of perfect lover gets quickly broken regarding popular media: If one's desire isn't heterosexual, isn't monogamous, isn't gender conforming, and so on. However, at the end of the day, if one can identify as the addressee of a mainstream love song, then on some level, one has to disavow the genericness of being interpellated as not a specific person, but as a mere consumer. Further, if this speaks to one's desire in general, one has to disavow unless one is perfectly fine with being loved for no particular reason at all, as would be the literal case in a situation of unconditional love. A condition is a reason, so unconditional is for no reason. And this is why Lacanians think that there aren't objects of desire, but only object causes of desire. In a way, if love so defined is a fantasy, could it really ever take an object? Could you be, could you be, could you be loved? That question isn't ever answered, for what if the you of this questioned *you* is itself but an impersonal fantasy on the part of the lover? Say something; say something … Some songs can take a different turn if you listen to them not high.

Why Are Many Songs Unfinished Love Songs?

A few weeks into living together, the love of my life asked me to play something for her. "Sure," I said, "and now that you mention it, I've been trying to write you a song. I sneak away at night when you're asleep. I use my headphones." I sat at the piano. "You know, it isn't finished yet—it's really just a work in progress more than anything—but do you want to hear it?" My invitation was deliberately sheepish, but the encouragement was enthusiastic. "You sure? Okay, here goes, then … I'm sometimes shy, but okay, okay, here goes." I played the opening chord and sang, "*Jasmine* … So yeah … That's what I have so far. But that's definitely the first chord, and that's probably the first word. What do you think? It's good, right?" Anyway, I always think my jokes are funny. To this day, though, it's still a one-chord and one-word song. Kidding aside, it's much easier to write something *for* someone than it is *to* someone. A gift for someone says, "I love you," but how does one communicate, "I love to you"? Really, I love *to* you is much more accurate. Not the dual relationship of an I who loves a you, the relationship is always tripartite, for there's an I, and love, and you. Someone isn't so much the object of one's love as they are the recipient of it. In *Seminar XX*, Lacan puts it this way also: "Perhaps someone here remembers that I once spoke of a language in which one would say, 'I love to you,' that language modeling itself better than others on the indirect character of that attack called love" (104).

Here, I'm reminded of something Kitrina Douglas writes:

> In recent years what seems to provoke me to create a song or poem, is that I have something I need (or want) to share, as opposed to a belief that I am a "good" song writer, guitarist, or singer looking for a "hook" to entertain an audience. Often what it is (that I want or need to share) isn't revealed to me until I start writing or performing, and in this regard I can be as shocked, surprised, or informed as an audience member at the power of a song to convey meaning or to communicate knowledge.
>
> (530)

Rather than from a lack in our being, from a wanting to be a good writer of songs, guitar player, or singer, when we pursue the artistic, isn't this but a wanting to share something that we hadn't heretofore known we had? Such is the idea of *poiesis*. Through *poiesis*, we bring something forth from nothing. To now switch to Latin, we create, in other words, *ex nihilo*.

What is it to create from nothing? To create from nothing isn't to create from the void. Nothing isn't the same as the void inasmuch as the void is all and only non-being. We find nothing, however, in the undifferentiated there that is. Nothing is what there is when that there is isn't divided up into things. When the world isn't divided up into things and is the great gemish of a one without even a two, then this state of no things is the origin of nothing. Stuff is there, but no things are communicated as things as such. The nothing is just what's yet to be communicated, what's yet to come into presence through the division of a language negating this thing, not that. Like someone you don't perceive in the cafe, the nothing is what's yet to emerge through the making of meaning. So, to create from nothing is to choose from the entirety of the world what to communicate. There's a lot to choose from. So, if we wish to write a song not simply to entertain, if we wish to communicate something that even we ourselves know not yet, it must be that it's the want to share that's strong.

We sometimes see that writers of songs, guitarists of guitars, and so on and so forth are people who seek fame. In at least some sense, people who seek fame seek to be esteemed. One who seeks fame seeks to be esteemed not by anyone in particular necessarily, but by a faceless everyone. Such is the pop star. Popularity is what's key. When we think of someone as an artist, we're typically thinking of someone who simply wants to create because there's a compulsion to share. To seek popularity is to ask, "Who am I with regard to your desire?" To wish to share an artistic creation, to share from *poiesis*, is to wish to give something that one doesn't have. For me, love is as poetry. And I think that this is what makes the artistic product, as opposed to the product made for popular consumption only, much more valuable. Sure, one can say that there's more aesthetic value in the former than the latter, but that's not to say that this is always true. For instance, Beyoncé's "Single Ladies" is actually musically complex if you break it down. Like one of my favorite jazz tunes, Grant Green's "Idle Moments," harmonically, it seems to at times slip into the symmetrical mixolydian ♭6, which gives it both a simultaneous major and minor feel. Still, for whatever musical value that "Single Ladies" has, it probably isn't as meaningful as a three-chord song composed for you in particular by a loved one with a guitar. When someone makes you art, it's valuable inasmuch as it's often a communication of I love to you: You, the recipient of my song, are the recipient of my love. And why are these songs often just works in progress? They aren't ever finished because the person creating them can't ever exhaust all the possibilities of their love. How do I love thee? Let me count the apparently innumerable ways, for should it be better after death, then my love extends even beyond my own being, something that I don't have if ever there was such a thing. And what can I communicate to you about you? Only one word seems adequate: no other word but the rigid designator of all your possible properties in all possible worlds, your name. Perhaps unconditional love is better framed as a love as it pertains to whatever being, one that's caused by whatever is loveable in you, but is what's at the same time more than you, for it also accounts for whatever you might become.

The Gaze of Self-Surveillance and The Lacanian Definition of Love

In "'I Know I'm Unlovable': Desperation, Dislocation, Despair, and Discourse on the Academic Job Hunt," Andrew F. Herrmann writes this:

> Instead, we look at ourselves. When *we* look at ourselves through the lens of the academic success narrative, *we* conclude that there is something wrong with us. *We* are not smart enough. *We* aren't resilient enough. *We* have not tried our best. *We* are bad interviewers. *We* studied the wrong subject. *We* picked the wrong advisor. *We* did not work as hard as we could. The academic canonical narrative reifies the discourses of lack.
>
> *(254)*

How is it that lack can be reified, or in other words, how is it that an absence can become a thing? When we read this passage, we see that see that it's one about our academic identity. It pertains to how we're subjects in the academy. And we see that at least part of this process of subject formation is inaugurated by our being compelled to look to ourselves. We look to ourselves and see what we aren't inasmuch as we're what we failed to do or become. And this failure to become becomes what we are. But why should this be? Why are we to define ourselves negatively? Let's examine being through lack a little more closely.

If we think about being through lack, we might find that we situate this being through the concept of want. What can be wanted? In order for want to be want as such, it can't ever catch up to what would satisfy it. Why is this so? In a very literal way, want is directed by something that doesn't belong to us. If something belongs to us, we can't properly be said to be in want of it. If we get what we wanted, then we no longer want it, but enjoy having it. True, once we obtain something directing our want, we may still have a want to keep it, but here, too, we see how want is driven by lack. When I have want pertaining to something belonging to me, what I want is to avoid its loss, so the want really isn't of the not having of the object pertaining to want, but now something driven by not losing. In this sense, we can say that the object pertaining to want isn't really the object *of* want, but the object cause of want. When we don't have something, the thing directing our want causes our want in terms of driving it. Further, should we ever catch up to the thing driving our want, that thing becomes not an object that we caught up to, but something that again slips away in terms of it becoming something toward which we might experience anxiety about losing. Here, it's also an object cause of want, want itself transforming into a want to not lose. So, in both instances, our want is directed toward a lack. First, it's a lack regarding the object cause of our want. Then, if we catch up to the object cause, it remains an object cause, for our want is directed by the negation of lack. But this is only to have explained the concept of want. How is it that want pertains to our being?

As we've shown, want always only pertains to lack, so if we want to be something, then we're saying that there's a lack in our being. A want to be means that we judge our being as something that isn't what we feel it should become. I want to be this or that means that we're neither this nor that. And what happens if ever we should achieve and become what we want to be? If a want to be follows the trajectory of want in general, then that means catching up to what we wanted to be means that that thing slips away from us. The thing that we want to be can never belong to us because want must always pertain to a loss. When we think we've caught up to what we wanted to be, then is it that our want is transformed into a want to not lose whatever identity we've gained. We have an anxiety over our identity, one that insists that it remain stable. But our identity is and can only be one of becoming. Want isn't ever a game that we can win, so to speak.

And from all this want to be—from all this stuff driven by an object cause that's a lack of being—we see that a certain type of being has emerged, a being that becomes a thing from an absence, hence the reification. So, why should academic being be an exception to any of this if want is the engine of our being? Of course, we can never achieve success. Of course, we can never be enough. The only way to disrupt this is to think outside of want. And what's outside of want when it pertains to our being?

What's outside of want as it pertains to our being is pursuing our being through being-with. When we pursue being through being-with, then we wish to be in a meaningful relationship. If we judge a lack in our being, then we want to share even this. And what is this want to share a lack that we perceive in our being but love? Lacan puts it this way in *Seminar V*:

> There is, on the one hand, the position of the Other as Other, as the locus of speech, to whom demand is addressed and whose radical irreducibility

manifests itself in the fact that it can give love, that is, something that is all the more totally gratuitous because there is no support for love, since, as I have been telling you, to give one's love is to give nothing of what one has, for it's precisely insofar as one doesn't have it that love is at issue.

(363–64)

Love is nothing more than giving what you don't have …

Giving What You Don't Have … To Someone Who Doesn't Want It

Jonathan Wyatt and Sophie Tamas are wise to point out a subtlety about connection. Here's what they write:

> She continues, more dully. "I just wish it worked, that connection was some magical *thing* you could manage and cultivate and bestow, deliberately, without making a royal mess of things. Mostly it just breaks people's hearts" […] "But our hearts aren't just ours to mess with. We make other people bleed. Sometimes just by writing. Even in hypermanaged connection, like collaborative writing groups. It seems like it's all about intimacy and flow until it isn't."
>
> *(6)*

Connection *seems* as though it's all about intimacy and flow. It stops seeming so when the truth about connection makes itself known. So, there are at least three possibilities about the truth of connection: 1. it's neither about intimacy nor flow, 2. it isn't about intimacy but only flow, or 3. it's about intimacy, but not flow.

What's the law of connection? For things to be connected, it must be the case that they touch. Things that touch must remain separate with regard to retaining the boundaries of their own identity. Otherwise, if things that touch were to become one, we wouldn't say that those things touch, but have become indistinguishably fused, dissolved into one another, melted into one, and so on. We reserve the touching of connection for things that keep their identity, but are now in a relationship where their boundaries lack mediation. Things that touch through connection are in an immediate relation with regard to one another. But there's more to touch in connection. For instance, my glass may rest on the table—it touches the table—but it isn't connected to the table. This would make for difficult drinking. Regarding touch as we use it in non-spatial ways, I may get in touch with my contractor to pay a bill, but I'm not connected to them as a loved one with whom I keep in touch on a regular basis. Here, we might say that touch is a necessary condition of connection, but not a sufficient one.

Connection is a touching—touching things remain distinct—but also a joining with. Joining creates something with a singular identity from at least two in such a way that all things joined remain distinct. When one joins pieces of wood with nails, for instance, I may get a shelf. The shelf is something now that emerges as a thing, but the pieces of wood aren't mixed together as in a solution. If I remove the nails, I again have the planks. Similarly, if many people join an organization, an organization emerges, but the individuals remain just that. When two people join each other in a loving relationship, they make a relationship, but just as with an organization, they don't stop being individual persons.

So, with regard to the latter, in what way can connection break people's hearts? Why is it such that in a connection it isn't that it's just our own hearts that are ours to mess with? If in connection persons are joined, though distinct, why should it be that others become hurt with us despite our best efforts? Shouldn't it be the case if everyone remains distinct, that feelings don't become as they're fused? Why should others feel with us if even in the joining touch of connection each individual remains their own person?

Let's return to the three possibilities of connection. If 1. what we say about connection is true, that it's a condition wherein things are joined, but remain distinct through touch and 2. it's true that in connections people can be hurt as though they're one, with which possibilities would this be consistent?

If in connection, hearts can be broken as though they're one, then it can't be the case that intimacy isn't involved. For instance, that my contractor overcharged me might break my bank, but not my heart. We may have met each other in passing as I headed off for work, but we never really knew each other beyond polite greetings. Thus, if intimacy is a necessary condition of connection, then it can't be either the first or second possibility, but only the third: Connection isn't about intimacy *and* flow, but about intimacy and not flow. This is consistent with what we've been saying about the joining touch of connection. In a flow, there aren't components, but one thing that's made up of indistinguishable parts. So, would knowing the literal truth about connection solve the problem of the connection of intimate relationships? Can we say, We're all our own person here, so my feelings really have nothing to do with yours? With regard to the truth procedure that's love, we know that to speak such a thing would speak an untruth regarding our experience, even though by the laws of connection, how we've set it up seems as though it should be that all parties would be able to keep their hearts separate, so to speak. No, it must be that the troublesome part about connection has to do with flow itself.

Saying that something isn't about something can sometimes be an innocent thing. For instance, we could've also said that connection is about intimacy and not about overcharging someone for building shelves. Connection isn't about a whole lot of irrelevant things. However, to specify what something isn't as a definition is to mark the absence or negation of something as a defining characteristic. To say that connection is about intimacy but not flow is to speak a truth in precisely the way that Wyatt and Tamas had framed it. Connection *seems* to be about intimacy and flow. That it's about intimacy but *not* flow is what gives us trouble. So, here we land in a more nuanced place. It could be that hearts are broken when the precise truth of connection makes itself known: We're brokenhearted because we seemed to be one, but we were mistaken all along. Things that share the touch of connection through a joining are always already not the flow of a one. By definition, this has to be the case. And what's most heartbreaking isn't that our hearts are broken individually and independent of each other. It isn't this at all, in fact. What's most heartbreaking when a connection is broken is that our hearts are broken from each other as though they were one, but at most, they were but momentarily joined. The changing of a situation from one thing to another can be difficult, but not so difficult as the breaking of a fantasy. To mourn the loss of what apparently never was, this is the most devastating thing. If in love I must give what I never had, what happens if it turns out that in the first place, you never even wanted it?

Broken Connections and the Ghosts of the Living

Let's examine a haunting refrain from Tony E. Adams's "Missing Each Other," perhaps one of my favorite autoethnographies.

> "I haven't touched anything," he says.
> Time hasn't touched the space: swimming ribbons from 1987 still decorate the wall; with exception of the comforter, the bed is the same; the desk with remnants of grade school—pencils, broken crayons, stickers, scented erasers; a wood box filled with once-loved stuffed animal toys—a sock monkey, two Cabbage Patch kids ("Brendon" and "Veronica"), and Teddy Ruxpin, a 1980s "talking bear" who moves its mouth with the playing of a cassette tape. I approach the large bookcase and see autographed baseballs, an altered Golf magazine cover on which my face graces the cover, and five father–son golf trophies.
> "You haven't touched anything." I say, somewhat ambivalent.
> "Nope. I didn't want to touch your things."
> I try to make meaning of his comment, the untouched room, and us, as father–son. I sense that my father has missed me living there, of us being together.

I read a subtle beauty in, "Time hasn't touched the space." The beauty is subtle because we might be inclined to miss the literal meaning. The beauty, however, reveals itself when we think of what this means as written and combine it with how we'd read it figuratively on our first likely gloss. Things that touch are things whose boundaries are in an immediate relation to one another, in a relation where there isn't a mediating between. If it's the case that time hasn't touched the space, this is to imply that time could've touched the space. In fact, it's otherwise the case that time does not, as Ron Pelias might say, leave space alone. In other words, time could've been in a relation to the space wherein there's an immediacy. In fact, without an intervention, this is what would've come to pass. But if time hasn't touched the space, then this is to say that there was no such relation because something must've come between the space and time. This is how we might read what's written to the letter. When we read that time hasn't touched the space and understand it figuratively, this means that nothing in the space has changed position—save for a comforter, which is interesting inasmuch as it has to do with comfort—that things are in the same place. Now let's see what the superimposition of these meanings yields.

When we see that nothing has changed except for the passage of time within a space, and something has come in between the changing time and space, we're left to wonder what has come between? In the passage, we see that it's the father's will. The father hasn't touched anything because he hasn't wanted to. It's the father who's stood in between the space and time, making it such that time did not touch the space. And when we see the son reflect upon the meaning of this comment, repeating ambivalently the initial part of it, only changing the "I" to a "You," then the ambivalence makes us question something ourselves. The space is one that should belong to the son, the space is what would've been the home of the son were he to feel at home there. Thus, the father comes between this relation, too. Namely, the father doesn't allow an overarching time to intervene upon the space that could've also been the home of the son were the son to have felt there at home. If the father comes between this overarching time and the time of when the son could've felt at home, what meaning can we make of this? Here, we're left to wonder as does the son.

The father misses—is not in touch with, shares no immediate relation to—the son and comes between the time that drives change, petrifying a memory of the son's time in the space. And this needs to be done because the fact of the matter is that the son isn't at home there: the time of being-with for the father and son has passed, and as we find by the end of the article, perhaps it never could've been in the first place.

It's for this reason that I read this passage as a haunting refrain. Not only does the exchange repeat a year later in the time of the story, but the father makes a ghost of a son who's still alive. And how can one not be ambivalent about this? On the one hand, it's touching, but it's touching because what's missed is precisely the touch of being in touch with, and to replace this being in touch with, what's substituted is a ghost brought about by not allowing time to touch space. Thus, rather than continuing forward, the space is haunted by the imprisoning and eternal return of the specter of a person who's still alive, an unrecognizable specter going by the name of Anthony Adams, a someone who, according to Tony, is unrecognizable.

The Oppressive Intent of Bullying

This is from Keith Berry's *Bullied: Tales of Torment, Identity, and Youth*:

> Bullying renders victims invaded selves. The "invasion" I have in mind speaks to the "encroachment" or "intrusion" that personifies bullying, or the ways in which being bullied constrains and restricts the lives of victims. Indeed, bullying is "oppressive."
>
> *(150)*

What does it mean to think of victims of bullying as invaded selves? From Berry's definition, we see that bullying is a type of oppression, but the insight here is that bullying is an invasion in the sense of encroachment or intrusion. Encroachment and intrusion are both transgressive of boundaries, and such transgressing of boundaries are constraining and restrictive because to bully is to transgress the boundary of the subject. What Berry's formulation shows us, then, is that bullying isn't a distant form of oppression. It isn't similar, let's say, to the type of exploitative oppression that a distant government exerts over a colony once colonized. Bullying is more intimate. But what does this mean?

Bullying is a form of what we might call intimate oppression, an oppression that transgresses boundaries by intrusively going beyond boundaries that touch. Still, there are many types of boundaries that touch, so what touching boundaries, exactly, are involved in bullying? Are these boundaries the boundaries of one's physical being? We might think of what intrusively goes beyond boundaries that touch as physical violence. To be sure, some bullying involves physical violence, but not all physical violence is bullying. We wouldn't call, for instance, two strangers engaged in a bar fight, bullying. Further, we'd call this instance of physical violence one that's person to person. A bar brawl isn't violence, in other words, that's subject to subject, isn't a violence, for instance, that I may instigate over social media, something to which you then respond to in kind. So, while it can be the case that bullying can involve physical violence, it must be that the essence of bullying isn't a physical invasion, but something else. In other words, bullying isn't bullying as such inasmuch as it's only an invasion of physical boundaries. But if physical boundaries aren't the sort of boundaries that define bullying, of what sort then? The touching boundaries transgressed in bullying are the boundaries constituting the subject. These are the boundaries that bind our identities through communication.

We're subjects because of boundaries. In other words, the subject is a subject as such because it's bound by a circumscription, so to speak. We're recognized as beings of communication because we're bound by identities generated by communication. When we interact with other subjects, these boundaries of communication touch. The I that I'm recognized to be is the boundary within which I find myself, and this boundary touches the boundary within which you find yourself when we interact communicatively. But it isn't the case that these boundaries shouldn't ever be transgressed. For instance, when we transgress the subject-producing boundaries with mutual consent, when we share what we are through the communication of the unspoken, we enter a relation of communicative intimacy. However, when these communicative boundaries are transgressed without mutual consent, it's here that we have what we might call an invasion.

For instance, if you break the lock to read my private diary, though you're reading something that communicates, you're reading something that wasn't intended to communicate to anyone other than myself. This, we'd say, is an invasion of privacy. An invasion of privacy is a transgression of the boundaries of communication. Bullying is yet another such invasion. Because this is so, what we can also see at this point is that bullying isn't merely to invade the subject, but what comes to occupy the position of subject. To transgress the boundaries generated by communication is to invade the person. It's herein that bullying is an intimate oppression. Further, we should add that this form of intimate oppression isn't simply person-to-person violence as in our example of the two engaged in a drunken bar fight. Nor is it the subject-to-subject violence that occurs entirely in the medium of social media. *Entirely* is the important term here. Bullying is a form of intimate oppression perpetrated by the subject not merely onto another subject, but onto a victimized person.

Let's say you and I engage in a social media war, or we go back and forth with each other on a comment thread. With words, I violently attack you, and you lash back with equal vitriol. At the end of the day, there's a digital record of our fight, and while anyone is free to read our back and forth, both you and I forget that we ever had such an exchange. Like the bar fight, we wouldn't call this bullying. Why? We wouldn't because at the end of the day, there's a forgetting. This forgetting doesn't occur at the level of the now digitally archived, but at the level of the person. Our intention may have been to hurt and belittle each other, but if, at the end of the day, we were able to forget any hurt, then the violence was subject to subject. The violence failed to touch either of our persons. And this is what distinguishes such an exchange from bullying. Unprovoked, or for a time mutually engaged in, should any exchange starting out as subject to subject go beyond the communicative boundaries and harmfully touch the other person occupying the subject, this we might call bullying. Thus, bullying isn't just the harmful touching of another's body or another's nameable identity. Bullying is the harmful touching of the person by an oppressing subject. But why the oppressing subject, and not by an oppressing person?

Even should the bullying be entirely physical in nature, the intent of the bully is still to communicate a harmful touch, to communicate this harmful touch from within the protective layer of one's own subjectivity. One's intent as a bully is not for one's body to cause harm to the body of another only for the sake of causing physical harm. Rather, the intent of bullying is to communicate hurt to a person. When one communicates anything, one must do so as a subject. In the case of bullying, the act of bullying itself has the intention to communicate an evaluation. Namely, the bullying communicates that the oppressive subject should be nameably recognized as being a position more valuable than the oppressed person, a position that makes the oppressed person unrecognizable to themselves as a person of value.

Being Excremental

The following passage comes from Christopher Poulos's "Spirited Accidents: An Autoethnography of Possibility":

> Deep inside me, in that place where other, healthier people go for safety and solace, I kept a festering, rotting pile of shame. You see, when someone—my father, or even just your garden-variety playground bully—attacked, there was something in me that always believed that what they were doing was right, that I somehow deserved to be treated like so much dog shit. I came to believe that I was no better than a pile of excrement.
>
> (52)

How is it that we come to think of ourselves as the excremental in the context of being shamed? And why, in particular, can shaming make us feel excremental? The excremental is that which isn't only unworthy of contact, but that with which no contact can be made. So, as one who is made to believe that they are but an excremental human, one comes to believe that one isn't worthy of community, of being-with. We aren't allowed the touch of contact, so not only do we retain the excremental, but we become identified with it, at least when another shames us in a particular way. However, autoethnography is a way to resist this shaming, a way to resist not only others who would have us believe that we're excremental, but a way to resist a whole economy of shame. When we give the gift of ourselves, and it's turned into the excremental, we can use a writing that can't be silenced to escape. To resist the economy of shame through writing isn't merely to disclose that which we've been made to believe must stay secret, but to willfully subvert through exposing our vulnerability. This is the gift of autoethnography. It is a gift whose writing comes into being through reading, a gift that is passed on through citation.

Poubellication

Let's examine three passages in relation to each other. Here they are:

> I give myself to you, the patient says again, but this gift of my person—as they say—Oh, mystery! Is changed inexplicably into a gift of shit.
>
> (Jacques Lacan, Seminar XI, p. 268)

> We probably all remember the scene from Buñuel's *Phantom of Liberty*, in which relations between eating and excreting are inverted: people sit on

their lavatories around the table, pleasantly talking, and when they want to eat, they silently ask the housekeeper—"Where is that place, you know?" and sneak away to a small room in back.

(Slavoj Žižek, The Plague of Fantasies, p. 4)

We'd have less knowledge, less academic freedom, and less OA if researchers worked for royalties and made their research articles into commodities rather than gifts.

(Peter Suber, Open Access)

In the first passage, Lacan doesn't mention it explicitly, but he's speaking of the obsessional neurotic. Namely, in their own estimation, every gift the obsessional gives becomes not only devalued, but turned into something that must be thrown out. The excremental is the partial object of the anal drive, and is the counterpart, so to speak, of the other partial drive related to demand, the oral drive. The oral drive's partial object is the breast. And drives are partial because their objects are, and we can think about the partiality of their objects in the sense that their incompleteness revolves around their impossibility. Again, the impossibility of the excremental is that it mustn't be touched, that it must be abjected, and the breast or bottle itself is impossible inasmuch as it can't be consumed, only its contents. Here, the partial objects are ones belonging to abjection and consumption, belonging to excreting and throwing out and to consuming to take in. At times, these two drives become intertwined in consumption habits that are meant to manage what we must abject, consumption habits that seek to hide what comes to be our humanity itself, a humanity which is made to be shameful.

It's also worthy to note that the obsessional's question is an existential one: Do I exist? I make this joke to myself when hands-free, auto-flushing public toilets don't function properly. I wave my hand in front of them, yet nothing. I must be a phantom! Still, taken as something applicable to scholarly production, this becomes something ringing all too true. If we find ourselves alienated in our labor, so to speak, and the labor becomes who we are when we sign it over to the capitalist, then don't we find ourselves thus magically transformed? Doesn't this seem like why Lacan, *à la* a Joycean portmanteau, might've thought it appropriate to coin the term *poubellication*, something describing our publications as though they were at the same time meant for the trash? The point here is to write in such a way that the gift of our writing resists becoming nothing but the mute, abjected excremental. When this is done in the context of autoethnography, what's resisted is the silencing economy of shame.

In the second passage from Žižek, though he uses this to frame his now famous discussion about toilets, we can use it to highlight the strange reversals it describes. Particularly, I think about the oddness of the reversal as making an implicit commentary on the anal and oral drives. One is rude, the other polite, and it's strange to see these assignments reversed, but really, why should either be rude or polite? Both are part of consumption, only they're at opposite temporal ends of the process. What we see is that if there's something that must be hidden about the final stages of consumption, the first stages of consumption should be equally in need of hiding, if not more. After all, we wouldn't defecate were we not to eat. This fact is of course perversely disavowed. Waste of all kinds is always the abjected product of consumption, especially when it comes to neoliberal consumption. For instance, when's the last time you saw a dump full of e-waste, or the landfill full of carefully separated recycled products that the municipality was unable to sell to be recycled.

The third passage from Suber describes the situation of scholarly production, but from a way that disavows its own oddness by focusing on the value of scholarship rather than the conditions of its production. In scholarly production, we find a strange reversal of what's railed against in the standard marxist critique of capitalist production, at least as far as labor is concerned. For instance, rather than the wage laborer being grudgingly coerced to sign over their labor to the capitalist and being forced to buy it back to survive, we scholars partake in the opposite. We beg the capitalist to take our labor for free, feel lucky when this happens, and when the labor is fully gifted, we're all too eager buy it back, not because such a thing would satisfy something like a biological need or fulfill a desire to conspicuously consume, but because we find the research necessary to produce yet even more research to sign over for free. Further, research produced by publicly funded universities, the institutions allowing us to give away our labor by funding us, becomes put behind a paywall, so not only is the public having funded the research blocked from something that would've been accessible had researchers not given it away, but the public must pay for it yet again! This second part regarding consumption isn't so much a reversal of capitalism, but it is an example of capitalism at its happiest, a sort of double-whammy capitalism where the consumer pays twice. Yet it's surprising—at least it should be—that we marxist professors are all too willing to make this happen.

The Shame of Stigma

Here's something from Erving Goffman's *Stigma: Notes on the Management of Spoiled Identity*:

> The area of stigma management, then, might be seen as something that pertains mainly to public life, to contact between strangers or mere acquaintances, to one end of a continuum whose other pole is intimacy.
>
> *(51)*

Though I haven't actually seen my credit report, I must still have excellent credit. Though others balk when I report on how I continue to accrue higher and higher debt, I can still be proud. "For over 20 years," I tell them, "on each and every statement, my lenders have rated my balances as outstanding."

The shame of stigma must be learned, so if one hasn't learned or has learned badly, then perhaps one is blissfully saved from shame. However, how might we undo the shame of the stigmatized that we've learned already? Once something is learned, it can't easily be forgotten as though through a willful forgetting. Does one even have such a capacity? Forgetting isn't typically done as an accomplishment.

If, like esteem, we experience shame primarily in the company of others, then avoiding the shame of stigma rests on others changing the way that they value. In other words, the unlearning needs to take place on the part of the valuing others. Further, if shame is less typically experienced in the company of others with whom we're close, such as how Goffman suggests above, then we might say that we experience shame in an economy of values that is also available to the general public. But is it the publicness of values itself that brings me to feel shame? On the other side, I presumably know the values of those with whom I'm close, but if I don't experience shame in their company, then it can't be the mere knowing of values that brings me to feel shame. In other words, the mere knowing of values isn't a sufficient condition for me to feel shame, although it may be a necessary one. One might argue that I don't feel shame in relationships to those to whom I'm close because this relationship contains an extra something. But perhaps, instead, it's that this relationship lacks something. It lacks strangeness, the strangeness that's present in my relationship with the public. So, to feel the shame of stigma, I must: 1. know that there exists a set of values to which either I myself, my actions, or my thoughts don't conform and 2. that this evaluation of nonconformity is accomplished by strangers.

And this is no less true for the writer of autoethnography. The writer of autoethnography must challenge the potential sensibilities of a reader who might find the writing shameful. This is the subversive power of autoethnography, a subversion accomplished through a willful exposure of vulnerability.

Invulnerable and Vulnerable

Of the kinds of abilities, the ability to be wounded that constitutes vulnerability seems to be an odd sort of accomplishment. Rather than being an asset, it seems more like a liability. Of the pair, we might instead think of invulnerability as the asset. And while this may be so, we can still say that invulnerability is a kind of an inability. But all this is counterintuitive. Still, I'd like to maintain that it's nonetheless true. But to explain how vulnerability can be an ability and invulnerability an inability, we'll first have to explain something about the concept of ability.

There are two ways in which we can think about ability: 1. as a mere provenness in the sense that something has been demonstrated and 2. as a capacity or capability, as a provenness for which one has made room. Both types of ability are things proven, but ability in the second sense of a capacity only includes that which has been proven through the agency of the thing with that ability. Regarding our particular focus, we can take both vulnerability and invulnerability in both senses of ability. In other words, both vulnerability and invulnerability can be thought of as a mere provenness, and both can be taken as a capacity. But that still leaves us with the two counterintuitive combinations. Namely, though vulnerability as a mere provenness and invulnerability as a capacity make intuitive sense, invulnerability as a mere provenness and vulnerability as a capacity are more difficult to grasp. Let's explain all the combinations.

When first we're wounded in a way that doesn't demonstrate having made room for being wounded—in other words, when we're wounded, and it isn't our will to have been—it's merely proven that we have the ability to be wounded. We're otherwise there, and someone or something wounds us, and this is the vulnerability of mere provenness with regard to wounding. It's demonstrated that we can indeed suffer a wound, but not in a way that we've made room for it. Now, let's imagine a similar scenario with one difference. We're otherwise there, and someone or something is about to wound us, but instead, this wounding about to occur is thwarted through our own agency. Here, we've demonstrated a provenness for which we've made room: We've made room for no wounding. This, of course, would be invulnerability as a capacity for resisting being wounded. So, these two are the intuitive combinations. But what about the counterintuitive ones?

Let's first examine invulnerability as a mere provenness. Literally, invulnerability describes the state of not having the ability to be wounded. If we're limiting the scope of ability to a mere provenness, then what this means is that it hasn't yet been proven that we can be wounded.

Let's re-examine our example of vulnerability as a mere provenness. What's our state of being otherwise there before the wounding? It's a state wherein it isn't yet proven that we can be wounded. This is a state in which there has been no first wounding. This is the state we might call innocence. And what's innocence in this context?

It must be the case that prior to our first wound, vulnerability as an ability is something that hasn't yet been proven. In other words, we must first have been wounded in order to be able to pronounce that we're indeed vulnerable. And this only makes sense. We typically don't start from a wounded position. Typically, we're first innocent, harmless in the sense that we're as of yet free from harm, free from wrong in the sense that we haven't yet been wronged. It's only after having been wounded that we lose this innocence. Innocence is the state of purity, a state of not being blemished by things that may have wounded us. Thus, as far as abilities go, the state of innocence is the state of an in-ability, the state of un-provenness. It's a state where what's speculated as a potential isn't yet a potential, for it hasn't yet been observed as one. And herein, we see an unusual quality that pertains to ability in either sense: Ability reverses the usual order of potential and realization. Abilities can only become potentials as such after a first realization of having proven the given ability. Things usually start as a potential, then become realized, but not abilities. How so? It makes no sense, for instance, for me to claim that I have the ability to control the minds of squirrels before having ever demonstrated it. You might say, "Well, prove it." And were I to say, "Well, I can; I just never wanted to," then something is suspect. With ability, realization must come before we can pronounce a potential. I guess the old me who was a young boy was prone to nonsensical boasts. But returning now to innocence, if the state of innocence is a state of inability, we can show that invulnerability is really only the equivalent of innocence.

We often think that invulnerability is the proven ability of not being wounded. This it is, but invulnerability isn't only this. Unproven vulnerability, the state of innocence, is the same as invulnerability insofar as it can be used to describe the same unprovenness of being wounded obtaining in innocence. Thus, there are two types of invulnerability that proceed in order: 1. invulnerability as an inability, as an as of yet unproven ability to be wounded and 2. invulnerability as an ability, as a provenness with regard to resist being wounded. To fill in the gaps, invulnerability can indeed be an ability, but only if it's preceded by a proof of vulnerability, vulnerability itself being preceded by invulnerability in its original position of an incapability. Invulnerability as an ability must always be two steps away from where it started as an inability. Vulnerability is in between. Invulnerability as an inability is an incapacity. Typically, no room must be made for it because it already occupies the same position of innocence which is what's closest to our origin. Invulnerability as an ability is what we make room for, but first, room must have been made for vulnerability. Thus, should the ability of invulnerability be sought, we must have first been shown to be vulnerable.

Shame Sells, Willfully Exposed Vulnerability Subverts

Here's this from Emmanuel Levinas's *On Escape*:

> Shame arises each time we are unable to make others forget our basic nudity. It is related to everything we would like to hide and that we cannot bury or cover up ... It is therefore our intimacy, that is our presence to ourselves, that is shameful.
>
> *(64–65)*

To wax somewhat Žižekian, if under capitalism, we've grown brazen to the fact that the emperor has no clothes, are we not sometimes scandalized by the fact that under all of our clothes, we ourselves are completely naked? In other words, why is it that as a consumer of US media, I can voyeuristically watch intimate relationships unfold mostly disastrously on *The Bachelor In Paradise*, yet still be uncomfortable when others come to know my own intimate, all-too-human pleasures, pleasures such as watching *The Bachelor In Paradise*? Only I can know that I watch that show, and I'm not even fully okay with knowing that all to myself either. The show is beneath me, for there wasn't a good place to drill a mounting bracket in our bedroom.

Guilty pleasure reality TV is nothing but shame made consumable. The shame of others is a valuable commodity for those of us who find ourselves inescapably caught up in an economy of shame, for those of us who are still also Victorians. It isn't good for capitalism for any of us to be boldly unclothed before the other, yes, because of the need to buy needlessly expensive branded clothes, but really, being unclothed before the other in terms of being human before the other, being human in the same way that one is intimately human before oneself. Capitalism convinces us that our needy vulnerabilities are shameful, and then it sells us things that promise to hide our vulnerability when others are around: The air around you smells human, so here are deodorizers to mask your scent, and were you foolish enough to think that everything is fine, you've clearly gone smell blind: Fabreze!

If shame hadn't first been a thing, capitalism would've had to have invented it. Capitalism doesn't so much convince us that we should consume as much as we can because we're superhuman, and we're thus worthy of everything money can buy. People who esteem themselves that much don't need to prove anything through purchases. Rather, capitalism convinces us that we can appear that we're beyond our unshakably weak humanity only through consumption, and this appearance is the most we can hope for, and we must hope for this appearance because at the bottom of it all, our needy, human vulnerability is shameful. And what can hide our vulnerability more than pointing out the shameful vulnerabilities of others in the form of consumable entertainment? Look, capitalism says, at how desperately lonely people behave! See how they embarrass themselves when trying to find love? Cringe at their exposed intimacy so that you can be less present to the self-intimacy to which you're forever exposed, the self-intimacy that you're unable to fully hide, the exposure that you need to forget when exposed in your nudity before everyone else. But don't worry. Maybe no one will notice your pathetic, shameful vulnerability when other shameful humans are in the spotlight ... But still, don't get too ahead of yourself, for remember, you've been just like Becca when Arie dumped her. So, at the end of the day, you still need to hide behind commodities!

Capitalism makes us feel not at home in the world so that it can sell us palliatives that help ease the pain of our shame. Reality TV is but a small gear in the machine. And in this way, it's a guilty pleasure in yet another sense: It's a pleasure we're allowed in spite of our guilt, the guilt of experiencing our own relatable realities. We identify only to disavow that we do. It's a pleasure to fantasize that I'm not really like that, at least not entirely, for I'd never date anyone with Arie's haircut.

Amidst all of this, autoethnography is the antithesis to reality TV. Reality TV draws us in with its intimate narratives precisely because it presumes these narratives shouldn't be told. It tells and sells its narratives this way, with an intentional, sensational salaciousness. It's a peep show wherein we're made to feel that we're forbidden from seeing the very thing it lets us watch, all for the price of either spending our time exposing ourselves to ads or whatever a Hulu subscription costs. Being a peep show, its enticing, forbidden nudity is the needy vulnerability of the human. And that in order to enjoy this commodity, we must first be convinced that human neediness is shameful. Yet another cost to us is the degradation of our own being. Autoethnography, however, is the opposite. It narrates human vulnerability in a way that removes from the economy of shame the inescapable intimacy we have in relation to ourselves. It subverts the notion that being human is shameful, that the things making us most human must be kept secret. Unlike capitalism that convinces us that our needy humanity must be hidden so that it can make the argument that we should just buy more and be happy, autoethnography frees us from the need to hide. It does this for the purpose of convincing us that our humanity is worthy of being exposed. Through its disclosure, it tells us that if we needn't hide our humanity from others, we needn't hide it from ourselves. So, whereas reality TV is an escape that traps us, autoethnography allows us to escape in Levinas's sense of being taken outside. We're taken outside of the economy of shame when we allow ourselves to be human. When we read it, autoethnography is a writing that lets us do just that. And inasmuch as citation is a promise to have read a work, to cite autoethnography is to pass along the gift of the autoethnographic. To cite autoethnography isn't only to incorporate the autoethnographic gift into our own texts, but to partake in its subversive practice of opening the closed not through mere disclosure, but through the revealing of autoethnographic truths. This is open access in a much different sense. However, we should remember that gifts aren't things given from duty.

Not Sharing All the Meaning

From the story of our lives, we might carve out certain narratives. However, we may deliberately choose not to tell some things. Either we choose not to narrate certain parts of our life to others, or we don't narrate these things even to ourselves. With regard to the latter, we may either choose not to create a narrative for ourselves, or there's a hard kernel of our lives that resists any attempts of narration, and this comes to be what constitutes the repressed of trauma. Narratives have meaning, and what gets repressed are the empty signifiers that remain when we can't make meaning.

Meaning is always a shared sense. Meaning is, as we say, co-created. And, as beings whose being is given over as meaning—the question of the meaning of being leads us nowhere—what could happen if the loved ones with whom we've co-created meaning are taken from us at the occasion of their death? If our own being is given over to us through the meaning we shared with our loved ones, then we're foreclosed access to creating further meaning with—and thus foreclosed from being-with—these loved ones. It could be that the signifiers surrounding these loved ones, the signifiers that survive them, cease to be assimilable to narratives, for we create no meaning alone. The process of coming to terms with this experienced lack of meaning through the loss of a loved one is what we might call grief.

In this regard, I'm struck by what Timothy Matthew Lee Sutton has to say about this in "Heart Murmur":

> What happens in the theorizing of my grief? Is it therapeutic? Perhaps, but then my grief, too, becomes part of a theoretical currency traded around an academic realm, perhaps doing some good, but it is no longer mine. I resist this move. I hold on to my grief as it is all I have left of either my relationship, or my grandmother.
>
> *(459)*

As academics, to some extent, we seek to create meaning with those beings who are our colleagues. These colleagues can be those we know or the unknown colleagues who are the presumptive readers of our published writing. Theorizing has academic currency, as Sutton suggests, because it makes a universal out of the singular. In other words, one's grief can be one's own, but if we share this grief—this loss of meaning with others—through theorization, what we do is that we fill a void with meaning such that it can no longer belong only to us. We put meaning into this void by sharing in a theoretical way that can be exchanged—as through currency, as it were—with others. Sure, this can do some good, but then this transforms the loss of meaning of grief into something else. What does this mean, though, autoethnographically speaking? Don't we often think of at least some autoethnographies as attempts to narrate a trauma? Narrating a trauma taken in this sense of the term is to share one's loss with others. And in an academic context—and we shouldn't forget that published autoethnography is a species of academic discourse—publishing a narrated trauma is a sharing of the void of a loss with colleagues, some of whom may be our presumptive readers, our colleagues unknown.

Lacanian psychoanalysis, at least as I understand it, isn't the narration of a trauma. It isn't the giving of meaning to what becomes repressed. I'm a Lacanian by academic interest. That's not to say that other forms of psychotherapy aren't this. I experienced three years of psychodynamic therapy, for instance, and on some level, it seemed to me that what we were trying to do was to narrate trauma. Towards the end of this three-year period, it was also expressed that I might have something like Autism Spectrum Disorder, and I say *something like* because this was several years before the DSM-V. Maybe that's why this sort of thing didn't do much for me. That isn't to say that it isn't useful for other people. It certainly seems to be the case that it is.

What this is to say is that it's perfectly conceivable that there could be reasons why one doesn't choose to share narrations of trauma. It could be, as Sutton suggests, a way of wanting to retain something of a lost relationship of being-with for oneself. I don't see any problem in wanting this. It could be that this isn't the sort of thing one is capable of anyway. That's one reason why I think I can write narratives to illustrate some philosophical points that I want to make, but I wouldn't really necessarily call what I do autoethnography, at least it wouldn't be evocative autoethnography. I have a hard time understanding my own emotions, and this might not even be a thing I'm fully capable of. Thus, I wouldn't expect that I'd be able to have any epiphanies around it either.

This doesn't mean that I think that other people shouldn't write autoethnographies if they so choose. What it does mean, though, is that I recognize that when autoethnography is written and published, one should recognize it for the shared gift that it is. It can sometimes take years to develop a rapport with someone in a therapeutic context to be able to share the sort of things shared by autoethnographers in their autoethnographies. Autoethnographers who publish share with colleagues unknown. And what they share doesn't just do some good, but much of it. If this isn't to altruistically put oneself in a position of vulnerability, then I don't know what is. Still, I think Sutton is right to remind us of just what's at stake in writing autoethnography. It makes us appreciate the autoethnographic gifts we readers have available to us, but it shows us, too, that as an autoethnographer, it's also perfectly choiceworthy to choose not to share certain narrations if one doesn't want to. Autoethnography is a way of life that one chooses, but again, it's by no means a duty. As a hospitality, autoethnography isn't forced accommodation.

Accommodations

In *Narrating the Closet*, Tony E. Adams shows us through the narrated epiphanic moment how heteronormativity constrains the comfort of those who don't fit into its framework. Let's examine the passage:

> "I know. This is why I believe that once we, as gay people, get comfortable with our sexuality, we become selfish," he says. "When we're not comfortable, we accommodate everyone else."
>
> *(78)*

Were things to be ordered fairly, it wouldn't be the case that anyone would have to accommodate the comfort of others at the expense of their own, for in order for one to feel at home, comfort must be shared. When what we share with the other doesn't provide us with comfort, we may find ourselves bound to an unfair hierarchy, and if we're so bound, we must work to create an order other than something hierarchical. Throughout the book, Adams suggests that humans have the existential need for acknowledgement, and that love extends itself beyond categories. From this, we can draw the general conclusion that the love we have for the loved one isn't a love for this or that quality in that other, but something that loves another with all the other's qualities, *whatever* those may be. In other words, we love the being whatsoever of the loved one.

Being-with is an ordering that puts oneself in a situation of mutual acknowledgement with the loved one. This is the position of the strength drawn from being-with as such, for literally, comfort is the strength of being-with, the strength we have from the fact that we are with another being with us. Being-with isn't so much an accommodation, a making room for the other, for being-with isn't bound to unshareable spatial parameters. Being-with is what we can have through absolute sharing, the absolute sharing that can only be accomplished as we share time. If I need to accommodate when another doesn't give me strength, then it must be the case that I move myself from the space, or that I'm moved from it, moved so that the other might enjoy occupying that space. It's herein that accommodation can mean to be displaced. Being so displaced, one doesn't feel at home or comfortable.

Comfort as the Strength of Being-With

Let's have a look at two passages from Grace Giorgio:

> Claire walked down the stairs and sat back down on the couch. The pitter-patter of rain on the windowpanes comforted her as she leaned back and closed her eyes.
>
> (Grace Giorgio, "The Wedding Dress," p. 402)

> They retired to the living room where a bottle of wine awaited them. Smooth jazz filled the bare room—a couch, a table, a flat-screen TV, and a mounted pheasant were Jake's attempts at creating home comfort.
>
> (Grace Giorgio, "Gigi's Tipis", pp. 616–17)

Here, Giorgio gives us two epiphanic insights with regard to comfort. The first passage involves nature. What gives comfort is the sound of the rain. However, we should note that this sound is comforting as one is inside the home not getting wet. The second passage speaks to how comfort is approached through the arrangement of a home. If we're comforted by the suggestion of nature from inside our home, it's for the reason that we've built and we are allowed to close our eyes and think. This is what we might say with the first passage. In the second passage, what's comforting is that one has made the gesture of an ordering of a home. It's in the second passage that we see that it's the loved one who can give us comfort when we spend time at home with them, when they spend time with us, and perhaps for us through their attempts to create home comfort. I think this is given metaphorically by what fills the room. The room isn't filled with the couch, a table, a TV, and a pheasant, though those things were there, the room is yet bare. The room is filled with, rather, music. Music can only fill something inasmuch as music fills the time. It's something of time that's fulfilling. And so, too, is it with the first passage involving the sounds of nature. In both passages, it's the sounds that are associated with comfort, and thus comfort inasmuch as it's experienced when feeling at home is given as a time of feeling at home.

The Slow Time of Home

In "Exploring a Timeless Academic Life," Joanne Yoo writes this:

> Perhaps, we can experience timeless time if we stop measuring its flow through achievements. Without an awareness of these badges, will we finally be free?
>
> *(198)*

The flow of time can be interrupted by times belonging to what we make to be our world. Achievements are such world times. An achievement marks a time to which we orient ourselves as living in the time after. For those of us who make our home in the academy, the clock on the wall is a tenure clock, and certain achievements become our world times. This is the time after I've achieved this or that publication, the time after I've made it through this or that review, the time after which someone has esteemed me through a letter, the time after which I've made tenure, the time after which I've made full. And how is it that we're to orient ourselves to anticipated achievements, achievements that are necessary for us to retain a certain identity, namely that identity of professor? The orientation toward these times can be one of anxiety. First, what is anxiety, and second, what is the experience of anxiety with regard to the time when we feel at home?

Anxiety isn't the same thing, say, such as a fear. A fear is something that scares me in the present. What's outside the tent? It's a scary, scary bear. Anxiety, however, isn't something that is caused by anything present. I won't go camping because there are bears in the woods, not to mention ticks that can carry Lyme disease, not to mention snakes, not to mention getting lost in a way that we can't find our way out, not to mention then running out of potable water, not to mention who knows what! I'll stay at the edge of the park in the safety of the car, thank you. And why do I sleep uncomfortably in the car? Because I'm anxious about who knows what. Is it anything in particular? Not really, inasmuch as it can be any number of things or all of them. It isn't any one thing in particular. The object of my anxiety is something, but I know not what. And it's in this that we Lacanians say that anxiety is not without an object. It has an object, just not a determinate one.

And again, what's anxiety's relation to feeling at home? When I feel at home, I feel at peace. When I feel at home, my time is timeless. I'm not worried that I'll miss this time or that, for at home I make my own time, and when I share this time of feeling at home with others, we share these times and make what we will of them in a way that gives us comfort. When I experience anxiety, however, I'm not at peace. In a way, we can say that the experience of anxiety is precisely the feeling that we might be in for an experience that disrupts our peace. When will it happen? I don't know, but it could happen at any time. What will have transpired? I'm not sure either, but something might happen to make me no longer at peace.

So, if anxiety and feeling at home are times that can't be synchronous, for it's precisely that we don't feel at home when we feel anxiety, can we ever feel at home in the academy if we have anxiety about anticipated achievements, namely not achieving them? What if this or that article fails to get published, or if I don't make it through this or that review after however many years, or if this or that person won't esteem me through a letter, or if for some other reason that I don't make tenure, or if I do make it, but I don't make full? If we orient ourselves and who we are in our world in part to the times of the world, then such an orientation to achievements can only give the reasonable person anxiety. It's only reasonable to consider the possibility of loss with regard to any kind of achievement. We can't feel at home until we're guaranteed that our achievements don't matter. And if this is the case, then if the academy is to be full of reasonable people, then reasonable people without tenure are necessarily ones who don't feel at home in the academy. The academy is by its nature inhospitable until it fulfills its promise not to disturb our peace should we do everything that it had asked us to by a certain time. So, who are we to be when we finally make it? Are we fated to be those who are so much worse for wear after having experienced prolonged anxiety for the simple fact that we had been reasonable about the expectations we should have around achievement?

Maybe, but we could be less aware of the badges of achievement. We can recognize that we must achieve, and that achievement must be accomplished in a timely fashion, but the anxiety can go away if these achievements stop being world times. All that matters is that we put forth maximal effort. Having anxiety over what we may stand to lose in the future isn't necessarily connected to maximal effort. And if our scholarly efforts are oriented to bringing peace to the world, can't we stand to content ourselves with valuing the achievements of having put forth maximal effort, not as the markers by which we will have ourselves been fulfilled, but as indicators that we've made it better for others? We should put our world into an order that's other than to the times of achievement. If we've made others more able to feel at home, perhaps this is a way to feel at home ourselves. They can always deny us tenure, but if we've done something good, that's never a loss.

Sage Advice About Thyme

> A man of my acquaintance was at his most well-organized at the unhappiest period in his life ... Then circumstances brought about a change in his life. It began with his getting rid of his watch.
>
> (Benjamin, Volume 2, Part 2, p. 591)

What is it that we're doing when we attempt to put our world into order? This implies that our world had been at first chaotic. But is the world chaotic? One is aware of the concept of entropy, but in a certain sense, if everything is part of a causal chain, then the world is in that way exquisitely structured. If one has the wherewithal, one can give an account of everything that is inasmuch as whatever it is has been caused ... and yes, one is aware of Hume. Still, organization could be seen, then, to be in some sense a disruption. It isn't outside of the causal chain that accounts for everything, but it is a disruption of where the causal chain would've gone were a will not imposed upon it. Organization imposes order inasmuch as it exhausts certain potentialities by steering the closure of those potentialities this way or that. Organization is a bounding of potential by the will. And perhaps when we organize, we have the fantasy of making a small dent in what seems to be an almost boundless potential for things to go not our way. In this way, organization is instrumental. The etymology of the word, in fact, bears this out. We will organization because its end is aimed toward something we value. And though the organizations we choose to will upon the causal chain to build what becomes our world aren't always immanent to the things organized, the modes of organization are always related to how we value. The spices in the grocery are alphabetized because they can sell with more facility when organized this way. Less minimum wage labor time is spent answering the question of where the vanilla is. And it makes sense that all the spices would be together and alphabetized within their own genre as opposed to being alphabetized within the whole that is the store. We wouldn't expect the vanilla to be after the tomatoes and before the watermelons, although Garcia Lorca is unexpectedly there if this particular imaginary supermarket is in California. In any case, my spices aren't alphabetized, but organized by flavor and frequency of use. Organization emerges from how we value. I organize things in my home according to the way I value, not necessarily for the sake of capitalism. There are at least as many ways to organize as there are ways to value. Here, one might note, the collision of wills can sometimes cause yet another thing. It's sometimes a wise concession to let the cook organize the spice rack. Somehow, I was left to be in charge of the kitchen cabinets. While I had no complaints, I hadn't requested that either. Was this a life lesson learned before our time together? I never asked.

As we've been saying, the home is an economy in the sense of its organization. Regarding this organization, there are the things of the home, but also the time of home. Time is always in chronological order, so it might not need ordering in this sense, but time does need to be organized in the sense that one must make time for this thing or that. More importantly, time must be made for the members of our home with whom we experience being-with. Like the spice rack, there are many ways to organize this time, for there are many ways to value. As a general observation with regard to these matters, the ticks of a clock might be like the alphabet: convenient outside the home. The time of home is perhaps better organized to the sort of time we've discussed when invoking world time, given, of course, that the times of our world are conducive to flourishing. Now that I wear a watch again, I take it off once I get home. It stays by the door where I keep my wallet.

You Can't Binge Watch Being-With

To have patience is to endure something. And to what is this thing to which we make ourselves endurant through patience? In the most general way, through patience we endure time. It's for this reason that I really like an insight that Christopher Poulos writes about in "An Autoethnography of Memory and Connection":

> But, with patience, I have found that memories can become stories. As an autoethnographer, I know what to do. I perk up, and follow the clues. I have learned to embrace memory when it comes, even when I don't like the first few steps along the path. I have learned to follow memory where it leads me.
>
> *(552)*

Why is it only with patience—the endurance of time—that memories can become the stories of our narrations? Sure, an experienced autoethnographer knows, as Poulos suggests, what to do. An experienced autoethnographer follows the path opened up by memory and lets memory lead. But why must time be endured first? Why, for instance, isn't an autoethnographer like the reporter who can report narrated stories with immediacy, without the mediation of time? For autoethnographic narrations, why must time come between, and why can't one follow recent memories closely on their coattails?

When we narrate autoethnographic stories, these are narrations of being-with, narrations of those with whom we've created shared meaning. In any situation of communication, it can be said that we create shared meaning, but inasmuch as autoethnographic narrations are meaningful to us as beings whose being is given over as meaning, we probably aren't narrating forgettable interactions that we have with others. For instance, I bought coffee today, and I must've interacted with the barista who understood what kind of coffee I asked for, but none of this is something that sticks with me. Such an interaction that's mostly forgotten probably wouldn't be what's represented in an autoethnographic narrative. Typically, what gets represented in an autoethnographic narrative is something that's memorable.

A few weeks ago, at an academic conference, my partner and I were meeting with someone who's proving to become more and more of a good friend as time goes by, a person with whom we feel more and more at home. The three of us had coffee, so to speak. We were at least around a place where coffee was sold. As it happens with those of us who work in academe, we sometimes develop good friendships with people with whom we have limited face-to-face interactions. In some cases, we're not only separated by miles and miles and time zones, but even by oceans. One might ask, Can we really consider people with whom we can only have limited face-to-face interactions, ones that happen only periodically, good friends? For instance, if I only meet a person once a year at a conference over a period of 30 years, then over a lifetime, I've perhaps spent less than 30 hours with this person, typical conference interactions tending to last no more than an hour. How close of a friend could this person possibly be? This is at least something that one could think. Still, it is the case that people who've only met once a year at a conference over a period of 30 years do consider themselves to be close friends. Why can this be so?

I like to think about this in terms of psychoanalytic interactions. A year of analysis might be around 30 meetings with 50-minute hours at most. People often report developing a close rapport with their analyst in less than a year, which would literally mean that much less than 30 hours have been spent in face-to-face time. Is this rapport, then, mistaken? Sure, that's always a possibility, but there's a difference between spending 30 consecutive hours with a person and spending less than 30 hours with a person over the course of an extended amount of time. The work of analysis isn't fully accomplished through the 50-minutes or less of face-to-face sessions. In fact, most of the work of analysis is accomplished during the time between sessions. As an analysand, perhaps what comes out in a psychoanalytic interaction sticks with me, and it's the fact that I keep returning to this thing over the course of two weeks that psychoanalytic work is accomplished. Thus, between sessions, I have two weeks' worth of psychoanalysis.

And isn't it the case that those of us who've taught summer courses often notice the difference of time between? Though contact hours must remain the same for accreditation and such, cramming a whole semester into a few weeks really tends to feel different because there's less between time. If we feel that our students get less from summer sessions, this feeling is probably not without basis. This would be the case just as much as you can't get a year's worth of analysis over the course of three consecutive days with little sleep, just as a friendship developed over meetings over years and years with much time between wouldn't be the same if you condensed all that time into consecutive hours.

It's often the case that in order for something to be meaningful, we need to make the connections between the gaps that only time can produce. Relationships to people with whom we feel at home are meaningful because these people stick with us even in their absence. And as this is the case for our relationships with other selves, so too is it regarding the self-reflection that sometimes occurs in autoethnographies that contextualize our former selves in the larger cultural context of being-with. Self-reflection—our being-with the self who is an other—only happens because there isn't an immediacy. Sometimes we must endure the distance of time to understand the interaction of who we were with who we've become. And this is why we can't follow on the coattails of who we are if we're to be self-reflective. Instead, we need patience to determine what of ourselves has stuck with us, to determine what will have proven to have been memorable. We endure time with patience, but sometimes this is necessary because it's only time that can solidify the plastic memories of experience into something that means.

Contact as the Sharing of Meaning and Time in Being-With

Let's consider two profound epiphanies from Ron Pelias's work. The first is a line taken from a poem in *Leaning*: "Our past is traced in carbon." The second is taken from *A Methodology of the Heart*. It's that "time does not leave space alone" (18). From these passages we can see two aspects of being-with: 1. shared meaning and 2. shared time.

First, shared meaning: What does it mean for our past to be traced in carbon? That which is traced on carbon paper produces multiple copies. Those copies come from a single event of imprinting, but the tracings form on different pieces of paper. In being-with, we share a history, and that history is meaningful, but it's meaningful in the way of that which is produced on the two pieces of carbon paper. In other words, there's but a single event of imprinting, but imprints that mean within separate entities. It's for this reason that we don't say the meaning of being-with is a self-identical meaning, but a shared one.

Meaning can't exist if it isn't shared. We know this insofar as signs must be exchangeable between a self and an other—even if it's the other who's oneself—in order to be signs as such. There must be at least two for communication to occur, for to make something common, it's implied that we first begin with two. In this way is it that meaning is common or shared sense, the *sensus communis*. Still, there's another sense in which meaning is shared. The famous question formulated in the opening of *Being and Time* is a question concerning the meaning of being, but as we've seen, Jean-Luc Nancy in *Being Singular Plural* reformulates this insofar as he asserts that being doesn't *have* meaning, but is, rather, given to us *as* meaning. Thus, if our being is meaning and meaning is something shared, it can only be that our being cannot be otherwise than shared, and it's in this way that we should understand being-with. Being-with is itself the sharing of meaning. For the human, there's no singular without the plurality of being-with. Put another way, it isn't as though we start with singulars and collect them to form the plural, but that we start with the plural in order that singulars can emerge.

But the problem is this: If being is given to us as meaning, and meaning itself is only shared, what happens if we aren't exchanging signs with the other, when we aren't engaged in speaking or writing? Certainly, we don't simply stop being. Thus, it must be the case that if our being is given to us as meaning, this is the being that's particular to us as humans. We partake in what's particularly human only when our lives are meaningful. If we aren't in the meaningful, we still are, only our being doesn't partake in human being. Still, is this to say that our lives aren't meaningful when we aren't exchanging signs with the other? Not quite, for there's more to communication than simply exchanging signs. There's of course also listening in communication. We can listen to signs in communication, but it's in the signal that we might solve the problem of how meaningful being-with happens when we aren't exchanging signs. But what's a signal?

Take, for instance, the fire alarm. When the alarm goes off, I know that there's a fire. The alarm, we can say, communicates to us when it sounds. However, so long as the alarm is functional, the alarm also communicates to me when it's silent. The silence of the alarm means that there isn't a fire. Signals communicate in this way. Not only do they communicate when I hear them, but they communicate also in silence when I'm listening for them. The signal is generally not how we regard the subject. We've also shown how, for Lacan, the signifier signifies a subject for another signifier. But what if the loved one is more like a signal? If our being is given to us as meaning, and we continue to be in the absence of communication, perhaps the absence of communication isn't an absence at all. The communication of being-with is simply not communication involving signs. The communication of being-with is the communication that occurs through signals. Not the subject that we find between signifiers, the loved one is between what's uttered and what's silent. The loved one is between the uttered signal and the silent signal, for with the signal, there's always meaning. In signaling communication, meaning continues to be present in silence. Isn't this why we can enjoy the presence of the loved one even in silence? In the silence, we experience a being-with that's just as meaningful as when we two are exchanging communications.

Second, shared time: From the idea of our past being traced on carbon, we can also see that being-with is the sharing of time. Recall that the meanings imprinted come from the same temporal events. In this way is it that time is shared in being-with. But what does it mean to share time? Further, is autoethnography a writing about shared time?

If we experience a time together, then we're saying that we're in a relationship with each other that goes beyond a mere assertion that this is related to that. The shared time we experience together is what we might call a synchronic relationship. Literally, the synchronic is together time. But is this together time the same as simultaneous experience? It could be, but were it only this, this wouldn't be in keeping with the way we're thinking about being-with. A synchronic relationship is foremost a relationship. If synchrony is how we experience being-with, then it can't be selves experiencing time merely alongside of each other, for here, there's no sharing in the sense in which we mean it. The synchrony of being-with is a sharing of time among selves in the sense of partaking. Is the partaking of time among selves durational? This partaking can't be, for to experience something durational is to experience something through time. Experiencing something through time isn't what we call the synchronic, but is what we call its complement, the diachronic, or in other words, this is why it's the past that's traced in carbon. The shared time is what we can call a history, one which includes the history of our historical present.

But why doesn't time leave space alone? Spaces change through time, so it stands to reason that the space of a home isn't a stable thing. Rather, the only thing stable about home is the time we spend at home. We might think of home as time, but the time of home needn't be experienced linearly, for this isn't to account for the memories to which we have access. Autoethnography records such memories, and it's through its narrative that autoethnography allows us to rearrange the economy of the orderings of a home, rearrange should things need to be reordered to achieve fairness to make room for the flourishing of all.

And what's this flourishing of all? It's the being-with of a Möbius strip onto which are written both justice and love. On some level, I see the present work to have been a book-length study in which I tried to learn the meaning of the last lines of Jasmine Ulmer's poem, "Critical Qualitative Inquiry Is/as Love":

> We might then contribute to a better world
> by countering the changing tides of our historical present,
> by teaching methodological diversity as methodological justice, and
> by teaching critical qualitative inquiry is/as love.
>
> *(544)*

3
THIRTEEN POEMS

Paths

Mist enjoys every moon month, and
yells into the eyes.
Such memories are year-round, but
night is a stranger to all waters, a stranger when
dark paints the purples heaven.

I'll perceive this voice
in the echo's morning, and
recalling the celestial waves cleared away black,
I'll have felt that
tonight, I had to go home.

Greetings, Stranger

If you want to know years, I'm surprised.
They can conquer everything.
Every day, the day is blossomed,
but it isn't ever only suffered.

The riches have been spoiled,
and we're here because we wanted it.
Freer and innocent,
I felt that my feet fell first into the world.

Come with me,
playfully, playing accurately, all too often.
Everything is what's said.
When I see the great, unbroken expanse,
I'm not at home.

With a pale heart,
I attempted at least once.
An inoperative machine
makes certain its devouring fortune.

Homework

They can't be isolated,
the three debts, but
it may be the universe,
images, your speech.

Though unafraid,
I can't fall asleep in the dark.
We don't have to dream,
especially at home.

Sweet Home Sweet

Good revolutions last and lastly
return me home to together see.

I'm drawn to you,
going forth where they love.
In the distance are the unseen colors:
The sweetness of home.

Now, we can do what we can.
Now, I don't care about
what flows frozen.
Only that immanent voice worries me,
to tell the truth.

Toward the Finite Home

Borders are mapped.
My bag and my held in my hands,
each arrival is settled
for poets and people.

Arrived, I want to be lost in the found.
Arrived at the home always running ahead,
it's here where we find accord,
waiting, and waiting, and waiting.

Calm for me is but an everyday,
but an interminable transfer,
not unlike bountiful smoke,
and volumes and volumes of images
that can only decay.

Breathing

I know you're not there.
You know everything I love.
You know all that you are:
Home.

And yes, we'll talk later in the world.
I'll ask about your life and where it's lived,
and you'll let me try your attention.

Why call out and bleed?
Your heart always listens,
but your thoughts are of blood and wind.
Is love, then, but air sanguinated?

Fugue

Like the page, they fled.
I don't know where there is.
Where's my home? Where is there is?

This child is necessary because it's
like the page.
This child is necessary because
I don't want to leave.

That's exactly what you want to do.
We said it every day,
"Yes, we know they've left."

Golden Hour

A light is broken from its favorite room.
Sit here in the window.
She turned the page, away from the useful, and
now we observe the revolutions.

The days of my captivity were asleep.
They remained entangled, and
with eyes closed, they ran afar,
aimed everywhere homeward
with the steadfast returning.

It's time for the immeasurable.
She told me the days.
Why? I'm uncertain.

Barbershop

I'm a young child, and I have a bit of money.
Maintenance should be my own.
We go there during lunch, and
I insist on talking to the barber.

There is my home.
It's everywhere,
and I only cause a struggle,
being everywhere away.

Two-color column,
the noon shadows further twist your words:
Here, I am at home.
Here I am, at home.

Fast Break

I know it's a dream,
but the Midas touched heart
is heavily golden.
Having to go from here
means not going home.

When things go well,
they aren't always mistaken.
Hear this song and never listen to it.
Leave alone.

The path is uncertain.
I'm on the way.
Many homes made, a dozen, in fact.

Taken into the heart,
I'm sorry about your
must be broken bones.
Bolt,
and one stays fast.

Borne Bare

His work has changed, and
as a son, he had a good week, but
I didn't.

The sea is beautiful.
Toast the ocean.
How can the voyage, though, be a maiden?

The mare is beautiful.
Give yourself a child's home,
mood, for me.

Please come back,
and you left you.

Carry-Out

Hungry, hungry,
ask the day after sunset.
Do you have any answers?

If you like,
begin with strength.
You can't avoid living ways.

Wait for me
at the window.
Who can answer?

I came home today.
You must choose a strange one.

We've come home today.
We won't return.
It can easily feed the heart.

The Long Way

By partaking, the home springs in me.
Are the festivities organized?
Take the steps, and don't give ground.

I have no skin,
have I?
Give yourself a child's name.

If it's a result, you'll be stopped in time.
Latent, the content isn't unrevealed,
but only the delivery.

Why do I apologize?
We're different, different from you.
Oh, enjoyment is more than naked winter!

4

THE DISCOVERY OF ONLINE DATING

A Happy Accident for Two Qualitative Researchers

Below is a selection of letters I wrote to Jasmine Ulmer at some point while I was writing some now long-deleted version of this book. Perhaps this is in keeping with the tradition of when they started issuing alternate takes of jazz songs on the reissue CD versions of classic albums. Digging through the archives, I discovered that these were apparently some of the first takes of things that would end up here. I was nicely encouraged by Jasmine to include them here for the sake of showing how thought can evolve, and that there's often—if not always—a lived experience underneath our philosophizing.

Just for context, Jasmine and I had started to collaborate on what would eventually become a book series, but then we ended up becoming partnered to each other along the way. Lastly, even though I was happy to share, I'm told that I need to take credit for the Glaser and Strauss allusion. She thinks most of my jokes are funny.

Subject: Co-Edited Project
  Dear Jasmine,
  Remember Words with Friends, that social media Scrabble game? I only ever wanted to play with the same 3 or 4 people. If Epistolary Novel with Friends were a thing, and we occupied an overlap in a Venn diagram long-term, that'd make me just about as happy as could be!
  I'm really excited to work with you, and the brevity of this note is inversely proportional to the immense debt I owe you for agreeing. Also, sorry for all the long emails. I didn't mean to write you a novel every time. Still, I appreciate all your thoughtful responses.
  James

[Several hours later]

Subject: Actually …
Dear Jasmine,
It was just one of my stupid jokes, and maybe this is just the way to late at night talking, but maybe Epistolary Novel with Friends should be a thing. You take a lot of care crafting your emails, as do I, so maybe we're actually doing a form of collaborative scholarship when we write each other letters. Why not, then, correspond in a Google Doc? Added virtue, it doesn't look menacing in the Inbox, and it can be read or added to without the urgency of email or the guilt of I'm writing you too much. We'd be just like Benjamin and Scholem!

As you know, I'm working on giving close readings to qualitative texts just like they used to back in the days of pre-New Criticism literary study. It's actually a huge project, like a 40+ authors over several volumes and years kind of thing. What I didn't tell you is that I haven't shared my work with any of those authors yet, and I hadn't planned to. I kind of gave the excuse of the whole post-New Criticism thing that the author is dead, and so on, but I'm kind of rethinking that. Scholars are people. It's weird that we have to say that, isn't it? Anyway, when I asked you if you maybe wanted to co-edit that volume and shared my work on yours as a kind of CV, you were the first author that I actually reached out to. I've really appreciated our exchanges—they generated quite a bit of thought for me—so I thought maybe I should suggest this. But then again, maybe this is a weird idea. I sometimes can't tell. Feel free to tell me whatever. I have a thick skin. I wasn't even offended when someone once called me *The Norton Anthology of Bad Ideas*. And that cut deep. Like, I'm not even *The Heath*? That at least would have a bit of dignity.

Also, isn't it neat how we were both in English back in the undergrad days? I don't run into many—actually any—literature folks in my discipline.
James

Dear Jasmine,
You remind me of Walter Benjamin unpacking his library. It's funny, these rituals we have around arranging our books. I have them, too, only because of my OCD, I have an additional layer of arranging them so the spines face the back of the shelf, the white sides facing outward. Though the books aren't on my walls, I know that some of my walls are books.

I like to see how writers think, too. What do you call those books that photographically reproduce the handwritten manuscripts? Those are great because you can see all the mistakes, and rewrites, and cross-outs on a facsimile of the page. I have one of those whatever-they're-called books of Benjamin. You know the first time he thought up the concept of aura was on San Pellegrino stationery? Isn't that wild? I mean, was he writing about that because of the paper itself? It's a couple of steps from bottled mineral water, but one could make the argument.

Anyway, I just think that's so cool, and you wouldn't have gotten that perspective from a non-facsimile version. Actually, is that what they're called, *facsimiles*?

And what if this were a handwritten letter? My OCD wouldn't have let me cross out a whole section because I'd have to start over. However, on my laptop, though the words are behind glass, I could just delete most of the *facsimile* paragraph because that's in fact what those books are called. But would that be against the rules of this whole letter writing thing we're doing? Should the words be unchangeable? Is that our law, the law giving unconditional hospitality to our thinking through writing? I mean, I correct most of my mistakes, have edited out many sections, in fact, but must some things stay put? It seems like they should. But can we sometimes Gordon Lish-style carve our own Carver? What kind of editing is still in keeping with laying bare how we think? Is it okay to simply simulate the trajectory of thought, or would that simulation degrade the aura, if, that is, it can be said that thought has an aura to begin with?

I know you're a not Joycean Joycean, and maybe there's a certain fidelity to stream-of-consciousness writing that we're trying to keep. And in that case, in the context of a fiction, it's okay to simulate. So, is the point of writing is thinking that it's also writing *as* thinking, meaning writing as though it were thinking? I always think philosophy should be that. And it's for that reason that I myself have an urge to stand up and shout, not to announce, but to reprimand—with good humor, of course—Why aren't you showing me how you think? That's the problem I have with academic writing by the numbers. It makes it look like we all think the same. When I read, I like to see the manner by which belonging to thought. That's what I love about reading your writing in particular, and now also about this project. The project allows me to see the process, at least from time to time, in your notes. Will these notes stay? Perhaps in the version history only. But it comforts me to know that they're there. Like Benjamin, perhaps I, too, have a collector's impulse. Do I hoard text? If so, can I be the Lord of the Files?

I'm going to set aside some time to re-read Barthes and Foucault on authors. It's a good yearly ritual, and I should partake in that. I might add Wayne Booth into the mix for good measure. Although he wasn't in conversation with Foucault, I think the notion of the implied author might be used to challenge the author function. Also, yeah, what's up with Foucault here? I feel that he wrote that essay for readers, so that we could rethink how we engage with texts. However, if that essay were written with authors in mind, then that's entirely different and maybe dangerous. So, maybe we should ask, Who is "What is an Author?" for? Further, while I get that his overall project is mostly Nietzschean—it being genealogical and such—and that there's a Nietzsche flavor to the exculpatory author function inasmuch as it's a "no doer behind the deed" sort of deal, he's particularly anti-Nietzschean in not reading authors as people. Then again, Nietzsche did this mostly to make fun of folks. Still, as you're suggesting, I think we as writers can hide behind the author function, behind the wall of books that eventually become our own *oeuvres*, publishing things with reckless abandon, not thinking about the wrecks we can potentially make when we position our own work's originality—and hence necessity—against supposedly dead authors who are our colleagues, colleagues who lovingly gifted us with their labors of love. Booth stops short of saying this, but maybe *we* shouldn't.

And of this we—of the we that's us, but also of the we which is the set of members of the scholarly community—if all scholarship is a sort of epistolary conversation, then we have to consider what makes up our we. It isn't the we of an I and a you—*you* in the capacity of a single other or totality of others—but the we of an I, and another I, and another, and another: it's all the I's in a relation of being-with with respect to each other, in this relation not as a collective, but as a plurality of singulars, all of whom have agency, none of whom are marginalized by being othered. That's how I read Jean-Luc Nancy's *Being Singular Plural*. *We* isn't just the sum of a first-person speaking position positioned against other signifiers, plus those other signifiers. I know, for a Lacanian, that's not a very Lacanian thing to say. I'm not being good either, I guess.

At any rate, you know the is/as of writing to thinking came to me because I've been arrested by your idea of is/as love. I've spent several happily productive hours thinking about whether or not to pronounce the "/" as "slash" or to keep it silent. I think the "/" *must* be silent because it's a partition that also functions as a non-semantic copula, if that even makes sense. Thus, the words need to touch syntactically, to have joint yet distinct functions because they only touch. So, were I to pronounce it, I'd merely pause, so the *is* and *as* wouldn't be interrupted by another word, but only distinctly joined by a silence between letters. In the flow of fluent speech, silence between letters, of course, has meaning. It means, however, without semantic interruption, its meaning being only to join what's to remain distinct. Also, whether you meant to or not, I think you might've invented a theoretical concept with the is/as, but I have to think that through more.

And might we not take the silence between letters in yet another meaningful way? When you read collections of letters with the immediacy of an all at once—you with Hemingway, me with Benjamin—it's different than having the experience of the people corresponding. When we're in the situation of some kinds of communication, situations such as letter writing, the silence between letters means. It means because, as you say, there's the time of thinking in between, for the time of being in the between of our letters still leaves us as interlocutors, though perhaps only in the sense that the you of the past stays with me as a haunting echo: you're *hauntological*, as they say. Joined yet distinct, epistolary interlocutors touch by keeping in touch.

It's interesting for the interlocutors of the missive because of this ontological situation. In fact, that's the literal meaning of interest: *interesse* is to be between. This project is interesting to me. I'm invested in it, and I'm honored to spend time being between your writing—as I have been even before this project—honored by your hospitality to have now been invited to spend time with your thoughts because, as you're sometimes urged to shout, writing *is* thinking ... and perhaps there's something to be said for writing as thinking, too. I don't know.

Lastly, I don't know why I compare everything to jazz, but re-reading our pairing, it reminds me of this Ken McIntyre album that has Eric Dolphy on it. McIntyre has a gentle, deliberate way about how he approaches his solos. And there's something about his phrasing that makes you feel that there's a whole world in every idea, however brief, and in between each idea, there's a whole universe. McIntyre plays the between spaces. I don't know how he does it, but he does. You go back to it, and you find something new each time because of what he's able to leave open. Dolphy is kind of all over the place. The only reason that his solos don't crumble is that he fills in all the spaces, playing too fast for anyone to really hear what's going on. It's a crutch, like hiding behind the books, something I've been trying not to do lately. I usually don't like Dolphy, but somehow he sounds okay with McIntyre's support. I'm not fishing for compliments, but it should be clear that you're the McIntyre here. This is just to say that I don't feel bad being the Dolphy because I'm learning a lot from you, and the value of that outweighs any insecurities I might have about writing in your presence.

Jasmine, as I continue to think about our exchanges, I keep finding myself wishing that doing scholarship were really this way, but then the immediate follow-up thought is, Wait, why isn't it?

James

PS: I'll see your Barthes and raise you a John Barth. Barth wrote every Friday for his *Friday Books* series. I think you might see me here with that same frequency, if not writing, revisiting what you've written thus far. Writing letters is a good way to relieve writer's block, and for me, re-living letters from a wise friend can do the same.

Dear Jasmine,

I have to admit, now that I've promised that I can treat myself here every Friday, I've been eager for the rest of the week to hurry up. It's not much of a wonder, then, that I got that restaurant, TGI Fridays, stuck in my head. You know, before, it used to be TGI Friday's, but now in the newer versions of the logo, the apostrophe's gone. Still, their slogan is, "In here, it's always Friday." Both of those things together are kind of horrifying. So, because the Fridays have become plural, and the slogan asserts that within the confining walls of their space, the Fridays are in perpetual succession, then there's really no ambiguity about what a space-time continuum mess that is. The weekend, which is what you always want to come, is perpetually deferred.

Say, maybe we should do a production of *No Exit*, but set it in a booth at TGI Fridays instead. It'd be exactly the same, only with garlic parmesan wings and spinach queso dip. That whole not having a toothbrush thing would be even worse, and hell would still be other people, only with an added dimension. And because you had brought that up in the context of *Waiting for Godot* and deleted scenes, when I read that, I briefly imagined what such a deleted scene might look like. If it were a movie of the play, say, maybe it'd be a post-credit out-take, like Godot wanders onto the set, and the director yells, "No, no, no! What's he doing here? Someone call security."

Still, I wonder what that would be for Beckett, I mean something deleted? What wouldn't count as being part of the text? Like the performative contradiction that's the name of *The Unnameable*, what would an untellable story be? And as you've been contemplating, what are the stories that *we* don't/can't tell? Why isn't what's sayable said, and are there many different kinds of silences between? Sure, there are already deleted scenes in *our* project—from editing, things said, then pruned away for clarity—but are there always deleted scenes in general because we must self-censor? Censorship often functions to uphold institutions, inscribing those institutions by creating borders of the unsayable, and for as much as academics claim to be critical of institutions, maybe we uphold things inadvertently, or perhaps accidentally on purpose. Because the unsaid often exists in between, what shall we read there, there between the lines of writing, but also between the walls of the social? And where, exactly, is the between of the walls? Is it a room of one's own, as in a single space between several walls? Or are they the between of plural single walls, as in just underneath the yellow wallpaper?

Speaking of, looking over what we've written, we mention walls a lot. That got me thinking about insides and outsides, inclusion and exclusion, and the interesting points that you make about these. I like your metaphor of the conference and how we all need to work to find the room we belong in, and to some extent we form our scholarly identity as we converse with like-minded folks. But then sometimes there are those of us who become silenced in these conversations, and it can be really, really lonely, especially when it's as though there are no others—no other I's—to converse with.

Then I remembered Badiou's book *On Beckett*. He says you can read Beckett's work as exploring these four questions, a Beckett list, if you will: 1. Where would I go, if I could go? 2. Who would I be, if I could be? 3. What would I say, if I had a voice? and 4. Who am I, if the other exists? (41). Beckett-like, I think you're asking that we think through these same things, only as scholars. And yes, I know, were anyone to be reading this, they'd think it a little too plot-convenient that you brought up the exact same questions in the exact same order. It's okay, though. We can share the secret that that's how it actually happened.

Lastly, by the way, I've been re-listening to that album. You know, I think Dolphy is tolerable in it because he's occasionally pulled toward McIntyre's stylistic direction. McIntyre is subtle, yet powerful. Subtlety can work that way. As you know, I'm prone to writing too much, just like how Dolphy plays in walls of sound, and though I probably can't completely change my style at this point, I am learning from you. For instance, as I was writing today, my initial inclination was to try to answer all four of the Beckett questions by myself, but then I realized that I'd actually rather know what you might think, and then I realized that I wasn't alone.

James

PS: So, I'm thinking some mean people in the academy are mean because they sometimes get stuck in that perpetual, never-ending Friday cycle. There're so many kinds of pressures keeping us from the weekend, and in that way, all only Fridays is hell. I might not mind the perpetual Fridays though, at least not now that I'm planning to spend as many of them as I can here. Also, I'm touched that you started writing me a handwritten letter. I'll start one, too.

Jasmine, very quick, impressionistic thoughts on your Anthropocene article in *Philosophy and Theory in Higher Education*. The only way I can think to praise it is in superlatives, but no one ever believes that kind of praise. Still, at least I can know that my feelings about it are just that. Again, just some thoughts as a first impression before I forget:

I think what you implicitly touch upon is the question of finitude. I think about this because I'm to some extent a Heideggerian. So, if we're stretched between birth and death, and this is our possibility—really the only one—then all our compartments to the world are toward death. Another slightly less Heideggerian way to think about it is that if our whole lives are a causal chain, then that chain, however many possible links get added to it, always terminates with us feeding the trees, as I like to say.

Then because I'm also a Freudian, I think about how all drives are death drives, and because I'm a Lacanian, how the meaning of life is the totality of forces that resist death.

So really, in a way, our concern with the Anthropocene is a forced repackaging of what we've always been concerned about: Dying. The only difference, as I was a child of the Cold War, is that we all kind of die at the same time. But my death is still my own—my ownmost possibility as Heidegger would say.

The problem we have with thinking about the Anthropocene is we're accustomed to framing it in an ethical way. The fundamental question of ethics is: What ought I do? Now for the entire history of Western ethics, at least, this question has always considered that this was an important question to answer because there are always people to come who'd also need to answer this question. In other words, ethics is important because the species of humans will continue.

Thus, though we all die, and we're beings that are finite in nature—being stretched between birth and death—what never dies is the species. At least this has been the assumption of ethics. Ethics, however, fails to consider what we do if everyone dies. In other words, the question, What ought I do? takes on a whole new meaning when there's no human future. And I think that's what we're struggling with. We're using a framework that makes an assumption that we can no longer make.

Now combine this with capitalist ideology. Capitalist ideology is a question not of finitude, but an assertion—albeit a very mistaken one—of the infinite. It's the infinite in the sense of Hegel's bad infinity, the infinity of always adding one more. Capitalist production asserts that we can always just have one more this, one more that, one more the other thing, and it never takes into account other self-organizing systems that it strains when adding just one more this, one more that.

So, here we are with capitalist production as regards scholarship: We're faced with this ethical question where we can't use Western ethics prior to this condition of considering what we ought to do when it looks like there being no humans is right around the corner, and we're doing it from within an institution that's been so suffused with the capitalist ideology of the bad infinity of an always one more. These things are incompatible, clearly.

So, where do we go? It seems to me that if we're to consider an absolutely finite ethics, an ethics for the death of all humans, then how we approach this question should also take into account the finite.

Now does this mean that we write less scholarship, that we don't succumb to the temptation of just one more article? At least in my opinion this isn't necessarily so. Why? For if writing is a human activity, then writing also ends when we do. The materiality of our writing might persist, but with no one to read it, it's no longer writing. And this is one way to interpret Hegel's idea of the end of history: The end of history is when communication is no longer needed. (Hegel might not come out and say this, but Alexandre Kojève gives it this read, and a bunch of the continentals were influenced by his popular seminars on Hegel back in the 50s.)

So, the question is, is it bad that we're writing about the Anthropocene? Yes, if we do it in a certain way that upholds the capitalist ideology of the just one more, but if we continue to write about it until we can't, and we do it in a way that tries to imagine the end of capitalism—in other words, one that challenges the ideological claim of capitalism that it's infinite—then that's what we should be doing.

Long way to say that everything in your article is, by my reading, right. The only thing that I might disagree with is your guilt. You're doing exactly what you're supposed to because you're challenging capitalism. Yours isn't just one more article for the sake of just one more, but just one more article for the sake of it being an important statement.

James

Dear Jasmine,

Not Friday yet, but another thing I've been thinking about this week is the books that are walls: Theory is difficult. But in academe, when we're around theory folk, especially the mean ones who weaponize it, we have to keep our ignorance a secret, otherwise we get shamed. What I mean is that in general, there's so much pressure on us as scholars to know everything, but understanding any particular theorist well can take decades, so it's really a steep requirement to have expertise in all the continental philosophers, say, that get categorized under the umbrella of theory. For example, I was thinking about your observation about what it might mean to be a bad post-structuralist, if there is such a thing. Post-structuralism is such a huge umbrella term. It collects together a bunch of thought from mostly French authors, but other than they're French and are thinking after structuralism fell out of vogue, they don't really share much doctrinally. So, for example, Deleuze is a post-structuralist, and so is Lacan. But there's so little commonality between those two for the reason that Deleuze's thinking during his collaboration with Guattari and after is a not at all subtle reaction against Lacanian thinking. The systems of thought don't share much compatibility because one is built on a rejection of the other. Both thinkers are exquisitely difficult, yet we're somehow required to know both if we want to be good post-structuralists. If it took a lifetime for Deleuze to become Deleuze, and a lifetime for Lacan to become Lacan, how am I supposed to absorb both of them, let alone that I'm supposed to absorb all the other French philosophers, too? Isn't being a good post-structuralist nearly impossible?

Also, we get all dicey when someone likes a different theorist than us. I don't know why this should be, but it happens. I mean, do you know? Initially, I was rehearsing in my head how I'd eventually break it to you that I was a Lacanian, but then you proved to be such a kind person through your letters, that it seemed silly to keep hiding it. Again, it's silly, but I was seriously contemplating pretending to understand Deleuze for the duration of what I hope to be a lifelong friendship. But really, how ridiculous is it to just keep nodding and pretending, especially when I can just ask you stuff? I mean, I get why people do that, but I'm glad we don't have the kind of bad rapport where if we ever disagree, we'd just start throwing out a bunch of incomprehensible jargon at each other—jargon that we know the other person doesn't know—just so we don't really have to engage or explain what might be unclear even to us. I know that sounds weird, but I kind of have that rapport with some people, and they're good friends. I know you use a bunch of thinkers that I'm either really weak on or don't know at all. So, can I just straight up ask you to teach me what you know about Deleuze, Barad, Manning, Ahmed, etc.? And when they're relevant to my argument, I'll explain Lacan, Heidegger, Nancy, and Agamben as best as I can. Jasmine, can that please be *our* thing, at least? And as I'm saying this, it sounds so weird, too, but why should it?

James

Dear Jasmine,

Maybe because you got me thinking about sports—that's a good metaphor, by the way, one that I'll have to keep turning over—but you know how people always say, "Go hard or go home"? I'm always like, Wait, we can go home? Yes, please!

It's funny where the first place our minds went with that question: Where would I go, if I could go? Until reflecting upon the differences in how we answered, I hadn't thought about how the question implies a potential impotentiality. All the four questions do, actually. In other words, the "if I could go" implies that going might not be possible, and if it weren't possible, that would mean that you're stuck where you are. Thus, either way you take that question, the "if" makes salient the place you're in already, and then it questions concerning your stuckness or unstuckness. A whole Friday later, is there still no exit? Most of the time, I'm not sure where I am, exactly. Do I have a malfunctioning hippocampus? Actually, am I *on* a hippo campus, a campus full of hungry, hungry hippos? And if you don't know where you are, it's a foregone conclusion that you're kind of stuck, stuck inasmuch as it becomes impossible to determine whether or not you've left. Still, that makes me think I should've also asked: Jasmine, where are you?

You say you had no desire to run away, yet you felt compelled to have a plan should that desire arise. I keep thinking about this, too. And this is what I wonder about your lack of a desire to run away, but your obligation to have a plan to. It's almost like a desire to have desire itself. That's vaguely Lacanian, but in a sort of unexpected way. I'm not real clear on how Deleuze and Guattari mean desire in *Anti-Oedipus*, like when they talk about desiring machines. And now that I can ask, I am! Can Deleuze and Guattari make more sense of this? Lacan can to a certain extent, and it almost fits a definition of desire precisely, yet it doesn't. For Lacan, desire can be the desire for the Other's desire. That's how it is for the hysteric, at least. The question is, Who am I for the Other's desire? Also, in general, desire seeks to perpetuate itself. But yours is like a lack of desire—we'd call that *aphanisis*, ordinarily, but I don't think that quite fits here—plus a feeling of obligation to have one in the midst of this lack. It's like, Well, I guess I should want this. I mean, I don't, but I almost have a duty to. And if I have a duty to—I mean it seems like this is what adults keep talking about—then I should probably study about how best to fulfill this duty, even if I still don't want to. Again, almost Lacanian with the superego imperative to, Enjoy! But if we're being absolutely technical, enjoyment and desire aren't quite the same thing. So, I'm wondering if that's where machines come in. Why are they desiring *machines*? What's the thing making them machines? Are they machines just because they are, or does something like capital or ideology make machines from things that wouldn't be otherwise? Your thing as a kid with its obligation seems functional almost, and machines seem more functional than driven, but maybe I have that all wrong. I'm not sure how literal to take Deleuze and Guattari. For Lacan, because the unconscious is a type of thought, desire is a type of thought, too. It seems to me, though, that for Deleuze and Guattari, desire is more of a product than thought—if a thought, more on the level of a compulsion, perhaps, but again, I don't know if I'm reading that right. And if it seems like I'm conflating obligation or duty with compulsion, we might remember that the *deonta* of deontology is a duty or obligation, but in the sense of a compulsion where one can't do otherwise. At bottom, in other words, with regard to the locus of desire, Lacan's unconscious is an unknown knowledge that's willful, but it seems that Deleuze and Guattari's unconscious is an unthinking thought that isn't.

For you, you don't want to leave, but you feel like you should. It's like the waiter just brought you the check, has cleared away all the empty mimosa glasses without asking if you'd like another, and is now pouring you water disdainfully. And that person who was at the dessert table: They weren't there for enjoyment like you were. Were they machining it, maybe? But you wanting to talk only about and taste all the desserts? Now that's Lacanian!

> Maybe it's this? But what if it's this one? Or that one? Oh, and there's this ...

Where is happiness? Probably in the place we haven't looked yet ... Or so we think. Is that why you like Seattle still? What if you go there? Would you just find that it, too, wasn't it? Can the disappointment of our not yets actually be the happiest place of all? If we've already gone everywhere and haven't found it—whatever *it* is—then that's the absolutely worst place in which to be. Then you're really stuck, because even if you move, it doesn't matter. You're just stuck in the entirety of the world with no place else to go. That being said, I hope to never discover that the world is where I don't feel at home, that I've just been in the world this whole time.

Still, I'm wondering if this is all sort of the way finding our place in the academy works. Also, might there be a being between the extreme ends of purposive and flexible? I think that might be where Benjamin's *flâneur* is, actually.

> Jasmine, where are you? Should you be here? Perhaps there? Oh, and there's here! Do you feel at home? And where would that be, where you'd be to just be?

And just like Dorothy, why do I, on the other hand, just want to go where there's no place like? If that's where I want to go, then that means I mustn't ever feel at home. You know, once, when I was at the mega-conference of my discipline, I spent a whole five minutes talking to this person who thought I researched the representation of black women in popular culture. I figured that they were probably mistaking me for another doctoral student in my department who did just that, but then after the discussion, when I was telling my friend about how I got mistaken for them, I realized that the person misheard me as saying that I studied Chaka Khan. So, that's my discipline and how much I belong. It made way more sense that I studied the one video from a one-hit wonder from the 80s than Jacques Lacan. This was at the job fair, and it was at that moment that I realized that I was so, so screwed. Anyway, there's a Heidegger thing for this, like a whole Heidegger thing, but before I think through that mess, I first want to know what you think about where you are, so to speak.

I know I'm holding us back from the next question. If you need to move on, I understand, but maybe don't get the waiter's attention just yet ... Just be, but be here at this brunch table, and keep me company while we think this question just a bit longer. And if you would, let's please have another mimosa. Because perhaps, in this moment of being between our letters, I feel at home ... "And you were there!"

James

PS: I'm so glad to know you're a real person who used to read the encyclopedia like it was *A Thousand Plateaus*, follows LeBron, went to Cuba, likes desserts, and apparently had a grunge phase. Remind me to tell you the story about how as a kid, I was like the autodidact from *Nausea*. My library didn't burn, though. My mom was buying one of those get a volume per week encyclopedia sets from the grocery store ... but she missed a week.

Dear Jasmine,

I realized that our friendship started with all the heavy stuff. Not that we need to avoid the heavy stuff, or can go back from where we are without that feeling artificial, but sometimes the heavy stuff needs support, and while close friendships are built on trust and sharing deep things, an important component are small things.

I think we skipped the small things. We got to know each other by basically sharing our deepest fears, how we thought we should change the world, our vulnerabilities, and all of that was right out of the gate. I'm not sure why this is. For a minute, I thought it was the letters, because we could go back and read between the lines, and that you in particular are so good at writing between them, but I don't think it's only this.

There's part of me that wants to pick apart our special rapport, and maybe that's important for something, but really, maybe we can just give ourselves some breathing time and enjoy it, at least from time to time. I don't know, but maybe that's why some work relationships get burned out. Some collaborators never get a chance to just go and have lunch together, especially now that we collaborate over these digital spaces. If all one does is work on a document together, then you stop being people to each other.

So, this letter is me popping my head into your office and asking if you want to go grab a bite. We'd probably talk about random stuff, and I'd probably tell you a story from childhood or something. Let me think of a good one ...

Actually, I'll just share a bunch from this project that was going to be called *Gary Childhood around 1980*. My birthday is '76. A bunch of the reviewers for my book project wanted me to include autoethnographies of my own, but when I tried to start to write them, they didn't come out quite right. You'll see what I mean ... I don't know. Maybe I'll just write a bunch of poems and see if that works better.

Focused Memories of Another Childhood

All my memories of early childhood are very hazy. Then, when I was about nine, they discovered that I badly needed glasses. Apparently, the very young Walter Benjamin badly needed glasses also. He got those and a specially prescribed desk. You can read about it in a vignette in the 1932–34 version of *Berlin Childhood around 1900*, one of my favorite books, for as Salvo asserts,

> All my memories of early childhood are very hazy. Then, when I was about nine, they discovered that I badly needed glasses. Apparently, the very young Walter Benjamin badly needed glasses also. He got those and a specially prescribed desk. You can read about it in a vignette in the 1932–34 version of *Berlin Childhood around 1900*, one of my favorite books.
>
> *(27)*

This ghost bearing my signature and I agree, at least on this ...

The Gaze

I still wonder about ghosts. For instance, are they material? For if they're able to haunt a particular home, let's say, they must be. If the world spins and orbits the sun, and if all of the universe is expanding, then how would it be that a ghost should be able to stay in place if not being subject to gravity?

My earliest thought about ghosts was a question regarding the perceptibility between ghosts and people: If ghosts are invisible, and one can only see them when covered by a sheet, could it be, then, that hiding under the sheets from ghosts was counterproductive? What if it were the mediation of the sheet itself allowing ghosts and people to see each other. Contemplating this in the dark, I threw off the covers. But what, I thought further, if I had gotten it backwards? What if ghosts and people were perhaps inversions of each other? It would be, then, that conventional wisdom was correct, that being on the underside of the sheet made people invisible to ghosts, just as being covered by a sheet made ghosts visible to people. Which to choose? After much deliberation throughout a sleepless week of indecision, I slept well: partially in the covers, partially out. If anything would scare away a ghost, it would be the sight of a half person!

Surveillance

Not wanting to fully endorse consumerism, the nuns made obsessively certain that we knew Santa was actually a saint. Saint Nick, they called him. It didn't take long for me to realize that I should be afraid of Santa, too: All saints are dead, and if the dead return, they either return as ghosts or zombies. Thus, Santa was one of the two. Jesus, for instance, was a zombie. We were told to be God-fearing, and I was. The crucified Jesus that hung on the classroom wall died a particularly horrible death. God was everywhere, so this was the Jesus I imagined to be in my closet, under the bed, behind the shower curtain. Had I found Jesus? Thankfully, I had not. In fact, I was desperately trying not to look. But what about Santa? Because our home—a two-bedroom apartment—was without a chimney, I was told that he could walk through walls. Also, he saw us when we were sleeping, much as ghosts do. The evidence was clear. Why did I consistently run from the living room when left there alone? The tree was full of Santas. I was only comforted to have been made aware that Santa wasn't real. To my surprise, the other children I told were not.

It Was a Pat, Then a Slap

During recess, in the rectory parking lot wherein we were allowed to play during winter, they plowed such that there were what seemed like mountains of snow on either side. We'd climb to the tops of either and voluntarily allow our friends to push us down into the fluffy snow of the unplowed grass. Yes, unsafe, but I grew up in the time of lawn darts and yellow, moderately watered plastic strips spread across the lawn into which one would dive headfirst. Needless to say, many of us sustained at least minor injury, especially when the snow compacted from repeated pushings. Still, we were all delighted to continue, sprains and bruises notwithstanding. However, sometimes the game would suddenly and apparently change to "I'll kill you, Salvo!" It was a two-player game, one for my playground nemesis and me, and only half of us knew it was a game. Though he was even smaller than I was and threw exceptionally weak punches—nothing, say, that could ever cause a sprain or even a slight bruise—my response was to cry out as though I was about to be actually killed. Juvenile justice perplexed me. Why did he only get five minutes at the wall for attempted murder?

Goose

But that was the old me, the old, younger me. The night before my first day of preschool, my mom tried to console me with the fact that I could use the opportunity to make new friends. Up until then, I hadn't had much exposure to other kids, so that sounded like it could be nice. As far as my extended family went, I was the first child to be born in the US, so any cousins would've been far away in the Philippines, and to compound the matter, my parents themselves hadn't yet built much of a social network. My dad only had the one friend from work. He had a daughter who I'd occasionally sit next to when both of our dads were playing tennis, our moms on folding chairs, sitting and talking by the sidelines. Sara and I had the job of throwing back the wayward balls. Neither of our dads were particularly good, and as I remember, one of them had to borrow a racket.

I considered Sara to be a good friend, a good friend, that is, inasmuch as she herself must've been remarkably well-behaved. For some reason, my mom would often pronounce Sara's full name, and though I now recognize her surname as being likely Middle Eastern, a homophonic confusion made me wonder whether or not I was being given an unsubtle hint: Why is Mom always saying that Sara had "obeyed"? Am I not doing at least an adequate job? I do throw back the balls, and that really isn't even my thing.

In any case, not wanting to disappoint my mother any further—having apparently not listened to her—on my first day of preschool, I took to task straight away. After we were all allowed to play together, I followed her advice and went about tagging people as friends ... And because I thought that I might be praised for diligent thoroughness, I went about tagging people as not friends, too.

"Your name is John? Mine's James. I just made some friends. Can we be enemies?" Lacking any prior training, my methodology had been modeled on duck, duck, goose ... "Sorry, I meant, Can we *please* be enemies? Thank you. Let's fight later when there's more time." But that was the old me.

Love,
James

Hi again, Jasmine!
I've just been thinking about the photo you shared with me. It made me think about meerschaum pipes. I only have two, but they're my favorite kinds of pipes to smoke because the meerschaum absorbs a lot of what a briar pipe doesn't. It's kind of like smoking through a Brita. Anyway, as you smoke a meerschaum, the oils and such from the tobacco are absorbed, and over many, many years, the meerschaum turns from white to this lovely amber color. Also, I think it was Stalin, but maybe Lenin, but either of them had wanted to gift an amber-colored meerschaum to some important dignitary, so he made a bunch of soldiers take turns smoking the same pipe day and night for several months so that the ambering process would be sped up. It's as though they hastened up the beauty that would otherwise come only from a slowness. I don't know how that pipe turned out. My guess is not great. You have to smoke a meerschaum with love, and with patient love. I don't know that a bunch of soldiers being forced to smoke would have this comportment. I'm sure they were just waiting to get their turn over, and if you smoke too fast, the meerschaum chars.

At any rate, why I thought of meerschaum pipes is how they generally tend to crack and what happens when they do. You can't smoke a meerschaum in the winter. The difference in how they heat up and the outside temperature causes microfractures. So, I was once at this antique shop looking at estate pipes—the fancy name they give used pipes—and I saw this wonderfully ambered meerschaum. The ambering was even also, and that's hard to achieve because the oils tend to collect in the stem by the bottom, but somehow this one was amber pretty evenly throughout. However, as I was inspecting it, there was a crack at the bottom of the bowl, and I'm pretty sure it was the type of fracture that would've occurred by smoking it outside in the cold. In any case, the crack in the bowl was more brown, but it was such that you wouldn't have been able to see it otherwise. Feeling across the surface, the crack wasn't noticeable. The crack would've been invisible were it not for the oils seeping into it.

I guess that's how the words emerged from the sidewalk also. My guess is that the salty water would've collected in the etching, and that this concentration made the snow melt there more than everywhere else.

That made me think of signifiers that are otherwise invisible until you add another element to them, like those notes written in invisible ink. The crack in the pipe isn't writing in the sense of someone having written it, but it's perhaps more like an index in how it signifies. It signifies that someone mishandled the pipe. I tend to think that indices, too, are a type of writing, just not symbolic ones. The pipe is scarred in a way. And while scars generally tend to heal and become more invisible over time, this crack only became more visible, and became more visible as the rest of the pipe came into its ideal, ambered form. The etching in the sidewalk contains a beautiful message, but it's only when it's covered with dangerous snow that it appears. I mean, they salted the sidewalk so it wouldn't be slippery, but the message only appears when they haven't yet salted enough.

It strikes me that both of these can be metaphors for how we think about different aspects of love. So, sometimes there are injuries that occur in otherwise loving relationships. Take the example of a once estranged parent, let's say, trying to rekindle a relationship with a child. Long ago, there was an injury that the child experienced when the parent emotionally mishandled them, so to speak. The child grows into an adult, and the parent is sorry for the initial emotional mishandling. And for years and years and years after having reconnected, that parent pours love into the relationship, but because that scar was like a crack in a meerschaum, all that love does is to highlight that crack. And the adult child doesn't know what to do because the contrast of the love given subsequent to the injury just makes that initial injury all the more salient. The adult child refuses the love, and the parent, feeling more and more guilty, gives more love, and you get this really bad cycle. If this sounds real, it isn't because it's autobiographical. I got along with my dad when he was alive, and my mom and I are really, really close. It's a real story, though, just not mine. Sadly, it's the real story of too many people I've come to know over the years.

Love,
James

Dear Jasmine,

You know, I guess you did figure it out before me, and I'm glad you did. Because I'm more of a phenomenologist rather than a materialist, I think about how there's a universe in every conscious being. If you think about it, this is true. I'm not just talking about how people are deep, and they have secret thoughts they hide away in the well of their heart. I mean, that too, but more how the world that you know to be the world, no matter how similar it may seem to my world when we discuss it, is still your own, and my world is still mine. I've thought this way for a long time. Strangely, it has to do with my vision, my literal, actual vision. My eye doctor sister thinks I may have mild tritanopia. It's the second most rare version of color blindness. For instance, I'm always thinking I'm dressing in monochrome, but apparently sometimes I combine blue and green without knowing it. So, if you're not color-blind, you see colors that I don't. For instance, what they call cyan is exactly the same as sky blue for me. I'm told, however, that cyan has a greenish tinge to it. I don't see it. In any case, though there's probably a world outside of my consciousness of perception that's the same world that causes the consciousness of perception of anyone else, that doesn't mean that each person doesn't have their own world, or universe, as I like to say. That's obvious to me every time someone says to me, "No, dude, that's green." So, at bottom, in each person, a copy of the universe.

And that's what I was thinking yesterday about my universe having seemed to have gotten a tune-up. But that didn't seem quite right. I think what it is, is that you complete me. That echoes in my mind so happily: You complete me. I know that people say this all the time, and I'm certain that this is a trope of at least 40% of 80s power ballads, but I never thought that could be literally true. In fact, around the time of my dissertation, I was developing this idea of incompletion, the idea that something incomplete could be forever closed off as such, closed off as non-completable, closed off as having the potential for eventual completion fully exhausted. That was at least semi-autobiographical.

And I'll now frame this philosophically, just so you don't get a toothache with too much sweetness; I mean, it's good to keep your teeth: So, as you quoted Richardson and St. Pierre, writing is thinking. True. Thinking is a fundamental component of who I am. True. You proposed that we write together, and I agreed, adding that we were same slating it on the piece of wax of a shared mystic writing pad. True. Thus, because writing is thinking, and thinking is a fundamental part of who we are as humans, then thinking together is that type of being-with that I wasn't able to fully theorize. I hadn't put it in this context, but the thinking together pertaining to being-with is actually just love. So, it isn't that my universe just got a tune-up. When we agreed to think together, my universe increased by the size of another universe. I hadn't known it before, but my universe wasn't *ever* in need of a tune-up. It just was incomplete, but not in the sense that there was a perfected incompletion as I had thought. I just thought that it'd always be incomplete because I hadn't known your universe to exist. I didn't ever even consider the possibility of your particular universe to begin with, so imagine how I would feel when you proposed that we share universes? Now everything seems right, and now I can have peace of mind, because now we share—with the full hospitality that makes available a feeling at home—our thinking. I had known philosophy's aim was to feel at home in the world, but it wasn't until I met you that I realized that you can't really be a philosopher if you're lonely, lonely even in a crowd of people. The smallest unit of philosophizing is something the size of two universes. And you had indeed figured it out before I did, but to my credit, I think I know it now, too. Thanks, Miss Art!

And I think the two components of universe pooling that you suggest are good. I hadn't thought to combine them, but yours is a really, really good idea. Carrying forth a tradition handed down from luminaries, but the ways we find for ourselves must include a component of teaching methodological diversity as methodological justice, with the ethic of teaching critical qualitative inquiry is/as love. Further, I think using the idea of charitable reading for what you've already been thinking is good, too. I hadn't carried the idea that far, but I think you're right that it can be used that way. Actually, I hadn't given the idea of charitable reading much thought. It's just something I knew got thrown around in philosophy, and I needed a placeholder for "please don't be an asshole while reading," but I hadn't realized the rich history behind the principle of charity until you brought it to my attention that it could have more life beyond that one paragraph that I wrote.

Anyway, I think Miss Art would've been my favorite teacher. And as far as getting to know each other, that's both a small thing, but also a big thing. I'm very happy that you shared that with me. I want to reflect upon this more, and I'll return to this in a later letter, but there are so many rich ideas in your narrative.

And just a mundane thing, something I wouldn't have paid much attention to before my universe doubled in size: So, as I was doing my daily Walmart walk, this time after lunch, I noticed a young woman pushing who I assume to be a parent around in a wheelchair. I can't be sure, but I think he may have had a stroke. As I was walking behind them both, suddenly the young woman spun the chair around and around, like how I remember the cotton candy guy got the cotton candy on the paper cone. He laughed and laughed with such delight.

Love,
James

REFERENCES

Adams, Tony E. "Missing Each Other." *Qualitative Inquiry*, vol. 18, no. 2, 2012, pp. 193–196.
Adams, Tony E. *Narrating the Closet: An Autoethnography of Same-sex Attraction*. Routledge, 2016.
Alexander, Bryant Keith. "'A Song for You'/'Killing Me Softly': Lyrical Dialectics of Design, Desire, and Disdain (A Performative Introduction)." *Qualitative Inquiry*, vol. 22, no. 10, 2016, pp. 771–774.
Badiou, Alain. *On Beckett*. Translated by Alberto Toscano, Clinamen Press Ltd., 2004.
Benjamin, Walter. *Walter Benjamin: Selected Writings, Volume 1: 1913–1926*. Edited by Marcus Bullock and Michael W. Jennings, Belknap Press of Harvard University Press, 2004.
Benjamin, Walter. *Walter Benjamin: Selected Writings, Volume 2, Part 2: 1931–1934*. Edited by Michael W. Jennings, Howard Eiland, and Gary Smith, Belknap Press of Harvard University Press, 2005.
Benjamin, Walter. *Illuminations: Essays and Reflections*. Houghton Mifflin Harcourt, 2019.
Berry, Keith. *Bullied: Tales of Torment, Identity, and Youth*. Routledge, 2016.
Bhattacharya, Kakali. "The Vulnerable Academic: Personal Narratives and Strategic De/Colonizing of Academic Structures." *Qualitative Inquiry*, vol. 22, no. 5, 2016, pp. 309–321.
Bhattacharya, Kakali. "Coloring Memories and Imaginations of 'Home': Crafting a De/colonizing Autoethnography." *Cultural Studies <=> Critical Methodologies*, vol. 18, no. 1, 2018, pp. 9–15.
Blockmans, Inge. "Encounters with the White Coat: Confessions of a Sexuality and Disability Researcher in a Wheelchair in Becoming." *Qualitative Inquiry*, vol. 25, no. 2, 2019, pp. 170–179.
Bochner, Arthur P. "Suffering Happiness: On Autoethnography's Ethical Calling." *Departures in Critical Qualitative Research*, vol. 1, no. 2, 2012, pp. 209–229.
Bochner, Arthur P. *Coming to Narrative: A Personal History of Paradigm Change in the Human Sciences*. Routledge, 2016.
Carless, David. "'Throughness': A Story About Songwriting as Auto/Ethnography." *Qualitative Inquiry*, vol. 24, no. 3, 2018, pp. 227–232.

Ceisel, Christina. *Globalized Nostalgia: Tourism, Heritage, and the Politics of Place*. Routledge, 2018.
Chawla, Devika. *Home, Uprooted: Oral Histories of India's Partition*. Oxford University Press, 2014.
Denzin, Norman K. "Indians in the Park." *Qualitative Research*, vol. 5, no. 1, 2005, pp. 9–33.
Denzin, Norman K. "Mother, Shane, and Sonny." *Cultural Studies <=> Critical Methodologies*, vol. 12, no. 6, 2012, pp. 500–501.
Denzin, Norman K. "Critical Qualitative Inquiry." *Qualitative Inquiry*, vol. 23, no. 1, 2017, pp. 8–16.
Derrida, Jacques, and Anne Dufourmantelle. *Of Hospitality*. Stanford University Press, 2000.
Diversi, Marcelo, and Claudio Moreira. *Betweener Talk: Decolonizing Knowledge Production, Pedagogy, and Praxis*. Routledge, 2016.
Douglas, Kitrina. "Signals and Signs." *Qualitative Inquiry*, vol. 18, no. 6, 2012, pp. 525–532.
Dutta, Urmitapa. "The Long Way Home: The Vicissitudes of Belonging and Otherness in Northeast India." *Qualitative Inquiry*, vol. 21, no. 2, 2015, 161–172.
Ellis, Carolyn. *The Ethnographic I: A Methodological Novel about Autoethnography*. Rowman Altamira, 2004.
Forber-Pratt, Anjali J. "'You're Going to Do What?' Challenges of Autoethnography in the Academy." *Qualitative Inquiry*, vol. 21, no. 9, 2015, pp. 821–835.
Freud, Sigmund. *Civilization and Its Discontents*. Translated by Joan Riviere, Dover Publications, 1994.
Giorgio, Grace. "The Wedding Dress." *Qualitative Inquiry*, vol. 15, no. 2, 2009, pp. 397–408.
Giorgio, Grace. "Gigi's Tipis." *Qualitative Inquiry*, vol. 16, no. 8, 2010, pp. 616–620.
Goffman, Erving. *Stigma: Notes on the Management of Spoiled Identity*. Simon and Schuster, 2009.
Harris, Anne. "The Way We Weren't: False Nostalgia and Imagined Love." *Qualitative Inquiry*, vol. 22, no. 10, 2016, 779–784.
Heidegger, Martin. *The Fundamental Concepts of Metaphysics: World, Finitude, Solitude*. Translated by William McNeill and Nicholas Walker, Indiana University Press, 1995.
Henson, Donna F. "Fragments and Fictions: An Autoethnography of Past and Possibility." *Qualitative Inquiry*, vol. 23, no. 3, 2017, 222–224.
Herrmann, Andrew F. "'I Know I'm Unlovable': Desperation, Dislocation, Despair, and Discourse on the Academic Job Hunt." *Qualitative Inquiry*, vol. 18, no. 3, 2012, pp. 247–255.
Hill, Dominique C., et al. "Notes on Terrible Educations: Auto/Ethnography as Intervention to How We See Black." *Qualitative Inquiry*, vol. 25, no. 6, 2019, pp. 539–543.
Hocker, Joyce L. "Turning Toward Tincup: A Story of a Home Death." *Qualitative Inquiry*, vol. 17, no. 4, 2011, pp. 325–331.
Holman Jones, Stacy. "Living Bodies of Thought: The 'Critical' in Critical Autoethnography." *Qualitative Inquiry*, vol. 22, no. 4, 2016, pp. 228–237.
Jonas, Hans. *The Imperative of Responsibility: In Search of an Ethics for the Technological Age*. University of Chicago Press, 1984.
Kavoori, Anandam. "What Is Peace? Being an Autoethnographic Account of Methodological Musings from the Beach." *Qualitative Inquiry*, vol. 24, no. 6, 2018, pp. 371–380.
Lacan, Jacques. *Seminar XI: The Four Fundamental Concepts of Psychoanalysis*. Translated by Alan Sheridan, W. W. Norton & Co., 1977.
Lacan, Jacques. *Seminar III: The Psychoses*. Edited by Jacques-Alain Miller, Translated by Russell Grigg, WW Norton & Co, 1993.

Lacan, Jacques. *Seminar XX: encore*. Translated by Bruce Fink, New York: WW Norton and Company, 1998.

Lacan, Jacques. *Seminar V: The Formations of the Unconscious*. Edited by Jacques-Alain Miller, Translated by Russell Grigg, Polity Press, 2017.

Levinas, Emmanuel. "Useless Suffering." *The Provocation of Levinas: Rethinking the Other*. Edited by Robert Bernasconi and David Wood, Routledge, 1988, pp. 156–167.

Levinas, Emmanuel. *On Escape*. Stanford University Press, 2003.

Nancy, Jean-Luc. *Being Singular Plural*. Stanford University Press, 2000.

Pelias, Ronald J. *A Methodology of the Heart: Evoking Academic and Daily Life*. Rowman Altamira, 2004.

Pelias, Ronald J. "A Story Located in 'Shoulds': Toward a Productive Future for Qualitative Inquiry." *Qualitative Inquiry*, vol. 21, no. 7, 2014, pp. 609–611.

Pelias, Ronald J. *Leaning: A Poetics of Personal Relations*. Routledge, 2016.

Poulos, Christopher N. "Spirited Accidents: An Autoethnography of Possibility." *Qualitative Inquiry*, vol. 16, no. 1, Jan. 2010, pp. 49–56.

Poulos, Christopher N. "Life, Interrupted." *Qualitative Inquiry*, vol. 18, no. 4, 2012, pp. 323–332.

Poulos, Christopher N. *Accidental Ethnography: An Inquiry into Family Secrecy*. Routledge, 2016.

Poulos, Christopher N. "An Autoethnography of Memory and Connection." *Qualitative Inquiry*, vol. 22, no. 7, 2016, pp. 552–558.

Salvo, James. "Intellectual Inquiry in the Age of the Efficient Network: Not Unpacking the Infinite Library with Walter Benjamin." *Post-global Network and Everyday Life*. Edited by Marina Levina and Grant Kien, Peter Lang, 2010, pp. 27–40.

Speedy, Jane. "Where the Wild Dreams Are: Fragments from the Spaces Between Research, Writing, Autoethnography, and Psychotherapy." *Qualitative Inquiry*, vol. 19, no. 1, 2013, pp. 27–34.

Spry, Tami. "Performing Autoethnography: An Embodied Methodological Praxis." *Qualitative Inquiry*, vol. 7, no. 6, 2001, pp. 706–732.

Suber, Peter. *Open Access*. The MIT Press, 2012.

Sutton, Timothy M. L. "Heart Murmur." *Qualitative Inquiry*, vol. 23, no. 6, 2017, pp. 458–464.

Tuck, Eve, and K. Wayne Yang. "Decolonization Is Not a Metaphor." *Decolonization: Indigeneity, Education & Society*, vol. 1, no. 1, 2012, pp. 1–40.

Ulmer, Jasmine B. "Critical Qualitative Inquiry Is/As Love." *Qualitative Inquiry*, vol. 23, no. 7, 2017, pp. 543–544.

Wyatt, Jonathan, and Sophie Tamas. "Intimate (Dis)connections: Research, Therapy, and 'Real' Life." *Qualitative Inquiry*, vol. 19, no. 1, 2013, pp. 3–8.

Yoo, Joanne. "Exploring a Timeless Academic Life." *Qualitative Inquiry*, vol. 25, no. 2, 2019, pp. 192–199.

Žižek, Slavoj. *The Plague of Fantasies*. Verso, 1997.

Žižek, Slavoj. "Ecology." *Examined Life: Excursions with Contemporary Thinkers*. Edited by Astra Taylor. The New Press, 2009, pp. 155–184.

INDEX

absolute sharing, being-with and 104
academic writing 120
Accidental Ethnography (Poulos, C.) 72–3
accommodations 103–4
Adams, Tony E. 90–91, 103–4
adoption 76–7
Aeneid (Virgil) 34–5
Agamben, Giorgio 5, 126
agency 51–2
Ahmed, Zahir 126
aletheia 78–9
Alexander, Bryant Keith 82–4
Americans With Disabilities Act (ADA) 55
"An Autoethnography of Memory and Connection" (Poulos, C.) 108
Anthropocene 31, 50 61, 62–3, 124, 125
anthropocentrism 62
Anti-Oedipus 127
archive searches 118
arts-based inquiry 32
authorship 4, 10, 41, 42, 119, 120–21
Autism Spectrum Disorder 102
autoethnography: *autoethno* of 24–5; autoethnographic knowledge, engagement with 10; autoethnographic practice 6–7; autoethnographic texts, nature of 8; definition of 10–11, 13; as eudaimonist discourse 64–5; evocative autoethnography, insistence of 67–8; 'I' as speaker and as reader in 12–13; insight into 4; listening to 10; literature and 4–5; living discipline of 8; lostness and 72–4; pathways for 59–61; philosophy and 5–6; *poiesis* and 8; psychotherapy and 4; reading autoethnography 7–13, 38; as a resistance to silence 26–7; signifiers in textual situations and 12; subversive power of 97; theorization about 9–10; truth in, forces of 72–4; truth in, pain of closure of 76–7; value of 4–5; as way of life 13; writing 7, 11, 13, 25, 26–7, 35, 101, 103; writing about autoethnography 8–9, 13; writing called autoethnography 4–5, 7

Bachelard, Gaston 9
The Bachelor In Paradise (ABC TV) 99–100
background, identity and 45–6
Badiou, Alain 123
Barad, Karen 3, 126
Barth, John 122
Barthes, Roland 120, 122
Beckett, Samuel 123–4
On Beckett (Badiou, A.) 123
Beckett questions 123–4, 127
being and being-with 27, 87–8
Being and Time (Heidegger, M.) 11, 110
Being Singular Plural (Nancy, J.-L.) 11, 110, 121
being-with 11–12, 17, 21, 23, 25, 33, 40, 49, 82, 121, 134; absolute sharing and 104; being and 27, 87–8; binge watching and 108–10; communication of 111; community building and 29, 44; cultural

context of 110; experience of 47, 108, 111; home and 74; hospitality and 50; lost relationship of 103; meaning-sharing in 28, 101–2, 110–12; narrations of 108; quantum superposition and 69–71; self-reflection and 110; strength from 104; time and 91, 110–12; writing and 11–12, 33
belonging 11, 18, 24–5, 28, 43, 44, 47, 67, 70, 87, 95, 105, 120, 128–9
Benjamin, Walter 30–31, 35, 36–9, 107–8, 119, 120, 121, 128, 130
Bergson, Henri 75–6
Berlin Childhood around 1900 (Benjamin, W.) 130
Berry, Keith 91–4
Betweener Talk (Diversi, M. and Moreira, C.) 41–2
betweenness 29–30
Beyoncé 85–6
Bhattacharya, Kakali 45–6
bibliographic conventions 38
bigotry 54–5, 57, 59
binge watching, being-with and 108–10
Blockmans, Inge 25–6
Bochner, Arthur P. 64–5, 68, 81–2
Book-It! program. 69
Booth, Wayne 120–21
Braidotti, Rosi 3
broken connections 90–91
Bullied (Berry, K.) 91–4
bullying, oppressive intent of 91–4
Buñuel, Luis 94–5
Butler, Judith 3

Callier, Durell M. 57
capitalism 95–6, 99, 100, 107; capitalist production 125; challenge to 125; ideology of 125
Carless, David 69
Carver, Raymond 4, 120
causal chains 60
Ceisel, Christina 71–2
Cervantes, Miguel de 33
charitable reading 35
Chawla, Devika 47–8, 75
childhood, memories of 130
Choose Your Own Adventure book series 69–70, 71
cisgender 53–4
citations 36; reclaiming the past through 77–9
civil rights projects 17

Civilization and Its Discontents (Freud, S.) 39–40
clarity, pruning for 123
classic albums 118
co-editing 119
collaboration 118, 126; collaborative writing groups 88
collector's impulse 120
"Coloring Memories and Imaginations of 'Home'" (Bhattacharya, K.) 46
comfort, being-with and 104–5
Coming to Narrative (Bochner, A.P.) 81–2
communication of being-with 111
community: home and 52–3; make-up of 29
community building 52–3, 56, 58; being-with and 29, 44
competition 79–80
concern, process of 21–2
consciousness 24
consensus 24
contact 110–12
continuity, between of 27–8
craft 32
"Critical Qualitative Inquiry Is/as Love" (Ulmer, J.) 112
cultural context of being-with 110

death and dying 124–5; death as sanction for storyteller 30; dying 31–2; obligations to dead and being-toward-death 29–32
decolonization 15–17
deleted scenes 123
Deleuze, G. and Guattari, F. 2, 3, 6–7, 127–8
Deleuze, Gilles 3, 126, 127
Denzin, Norman 8–9, 14, 15, 77–9
deontology 14–15, 128; deontological ethics 18
Derrida, Jacques 3, 5, 48–9
desire 127
desire, relationships of 82
disappointment 128
disclosure 73
dissertations 2
Diversi, Marchelo 41–2
Dolphy, Eric 122, 123–4
Don Quixote (Cervantes, M.de) 33
Douglas, Kitrina 2, 84–5
DSM-V Diagnostics 102
Dutta, Urmitapa 46–7

"Ecology" (Žižek, S.) 61–2
Ellis, Carolyn 21–2, 23–5, 32–3, 34–5, 82
emails, crafting of 119
emotion (and emotions) 57–8, 68, 77, 78, 103; anger-emotion 28; emotional mishandling 133; writing about 78–9
empirical research 27
"Encounters with the White Coat" (Blockmans, I.) 25–6
epiphany 73
On Escape (Levinas, E.) 99–101
ethics 53; fundamental question of 124; of knowledge withheld 76–7; social justice, ethical framework for 14–15, 17–18
The Ethnographic I (Ellis, C.) 21–2, 23–5, 32–3, 34–5
etymology 21–2
Euclidean spaces 50
eudaimonistic discourse 60, 64–5, 68, 74; autoethnography as 64–5
evocative autoethnography, insistence of 67–8
exclusion 56, 123; exclusionary practices 54, 56; marginalization and 53–5
excremental shame (or shaming) 94
experience of being-with 47, 108, 111
"Exploring a Timeless Academic Life" (Yoo, J.) 105

facsimile 120
fairness 17, 19, 44, 51, 73–4, 112
family and home 46
Fanon, Franz 15–16
Fifth Amendment 15
filing systems 35–6
finitude 124–5
Flaubert, Gustave 37
Forber-Pratt, Anjali J. 27
Foucault, Michel 3, 73–4, 120
"Fragments and Fictions" (Henson, D.) 70–71
free will 60
Freud, Sigmund 35–6, 39–40, 124
Friday Books series (Barth, J.) 122
friendship 129; making friends (and enemies) in preschool 131–2
functionality 127
future relationships 20

García Lorca, Federico 107
García Márquez, Gabriel 37
Gherovici, Patricia 55
ghosts of the living 90–91

"Gigi's Tipis" (Giorgio, G,) 104
Giorgio, Grace 104–5
giving (and receiving) 88–90
global warming catastrophe 63–4
Globalized Nostalgia (Ceisel, C.) 71–2
glory, focus on 58
Goffman, Erving 96–7
Google Doc 119
grand life stories 70–71
Green, Grant 85–6
grief in relationships 102
Guattari, F. and Deleuze, G. 129
Guattari, Félix 126, 127

handwritten manuscripts, photographic reproduction of 119–20
happiness 128
Haraway, Donna 3
Harris, Anne 76–7
"Heart Murmur" (Sutton, T.M.L.) 102–3
Hegel, Georg W.F. 58, 125
Heidegger, Martin 5, 11, 44, 62, 74–5, 79, 124, 126, 129
Hemingway, Ernest 121
Henson, Donna 70–71
Herrmann, Andrew F. 86–7
heteronormativity 83
Hill, Dominique C. 57
hippocampus 127
Hocker, Joyce 29–30, 32
Holman Jones, Stacy 5–6
home 40; being-with and 74; community and 52–3; family and 46; homeland and 46–7; need for creation of 48; peace at 45; place of 43; rules of 73–4; slow time of 105–6; time at, being at home in the world and 47–8; time at home 47–8; together at 23–5; in unfair world, justice and 50–53
Home, Uprooted (Chawla, D.) 47–8, 75
homeland 46–7
homesickness 74–6
hospitality 48–50, 53–5; being-with and 50
Of Hospitality (Derrida, J.) 48–9
human rights projects 17

'I' as speaker and as reader 12–13
"I Know I'm Unlovable" (Herrmann, A.F.) 86–7
identity 43; first-person plural and 24; formation of 25–6; fromness and 45–6
"Idle Moments" (Grant Green) 85–6
Illuminations (Benjamin, W.) 30–31

immortality 61
The Imperative of Responsibility (Jonas, H.) 62
importance, hierarchy of 63–4
incompletion, idea of 134–5
"Indians in the Park" (Denzin, N.) 77–9
infinity 125
inhospitability, unfairness in 51
insides, outsides and 123
interest 21–3, 28; betweenness of 22–3; meaning of 121–2; object of 22
interlocution 121–2
interpersonal relationships 19
interruption, between of 27–9
intersubjective relationship 25
"Intimate (Dis)connections: Research, Therapy, and 'Real Life'" (Wyatt, J. and Tamas, S.) 88–90
intimate relationships 89, 99–100
inverse proportionality, relationships and 64–5
invulnerability 97–9
itinerary time 72

jazz: comparison to 122; jazz songs 118
Jesus Christ 15, 131
job market 1
Jonas, Hans 62
Joyce, James 95, 120
justice 18–21, 53; concept of 15; juvenile justice 131; law and 20; methodological justice 135; rights and 56–7

Kahn, Chaka 129
Kant, Immanuel 14
Kavoori, Anandam 44–5
Khan, Chaka 2, 3–4
knowledge withheld 76–7
Kojève, Alexandre 125

Lacan, Jacques (and Lacanian perspective) 1, 2, 3, 4–5, 6–7, 12, 13, 16; being-with, home and love 81, 84, 87–8, 94, 95, 102, 105; Love, Lacanian definition of 86–8; qualitative researchers online 121, 124, 126, 127–8, 129; reading autoethnography 41, 54–5, 65–6, 67
lack 55, 85, 86–7, 88, 102, 127
law: politics and 19–20; prescriptive laws of governance 59–60
Leaning: A Poetics of Personal Relations (Pelias, R.J.) 110
letter writing 118–35

Levinas, Emmanuel 62, 66–7, 99–101
"Life, Interrupted" (Poulos, C.) 28
limited resources 42
Lish, Gordon 4, 120
listening to autoethnography 10
literary reviews 36–9; writing and 37
literary theory 3–4
literature and autoethnography 4–5
"Living Bodies of Thought" (Holman Jones, S.) 5–6
living discipline of autoethnography 8
"The Long Way Home" (Dutta, U.) 46–7
lost relationships 103
lostness, autoethnography and 72–4
Love, Lacanian definition of 86–8
loving relationships 89, 133

machines 100, 114, 127
"Make America Great Again" 18
man in the world, presence of 62
manipulation 51, 52
Manning, Peter K. 126
materialism 134
materiality 125
McIntyre, Ken 122, 123–4
me-against-the-world mentality 52
meaning-sharing 101–3, 110–12; in being-with 28, 101–2, 110–12
meaningful relationships 87, 109–10
meerschaum pipes 132–3
memories 39–40, 40–41; playground memories 131
Memories of My Nervous Illness (Schreber, D.P.) 36
merit, fantasy of 42
Merleau-Ponty, Maurice 78–9
metaphor 15, 16, 17, 23, 43–4, 73, 105, 123, 127, 133
methodological justice 135
methodology: methodological model 32–4; value of method 33–4
Methodology of the Heart: Evoking Academic and Daily Life (Pelias, R.J.) 110
Miranda Warning 15
"Missing Each Other" (Adams, T.E.) 90–91
mistaken identity 1–2
Mitsein ('being-with') 5, 11–12, 33
Möbius strip 112
Moreira, Claudio 41–2
"Mother, Shane, and Sonny" (Denzin, N.) 79
Mouffe, Chantal 58
movement through time 42–3

Nancy, Jean-Luc 5, 11, 110, 121, 126
Narrating the Closet (Adams, T.E.) 103–4
narrations of being-with 108
narrative 34–5
narrative arc 70–71
National Communication Association (NCA) 1
nationality 45
Nausea (Sartre, J.-P.) 129
New Criticism 119
Nietzsche, Friederich 77, 120–21
No Exit (Jean-Paul Sartre play) 58, 123
non-rationality 20

Occupy movement 16
OCD (obsessive-compulsive disorder) 119, 120
oeuvres 121
offensiveness 55–7
online dating 118–35
Open Access (Suber, P.) 95, 96
opposition, relationships of 64
oppressive intent of bullying 91–4
oppressiveness 55–7
originality 121
originary relationship 82

Parker, Pat 57
past as haunting echo 121
pathways for autoethnography 59–61
peace at home 45
Pelias, Ron J. 21, 25, 29, 32, 41, 60–61, 68, 90–91, 110
perception, perspective and 24
performativity 19, 73–4, 123
"Performing Autoethnography" (Spry, T.) 10–11
personal, political and 19
Phantom of Liberty (Luis Buñuel film) 94–5
phenomenology 134
philosophization 118
philosophy 3, 120; autoethnography and 5–6; on love 20; when philosophy class was over 57–9
Philosophy and Theory in Higher Education 124
Pinter, Harold 58
place: division and 44; fromness and 45–6, 49–50; of home 43; home as place of peace 42–5; placed things and 44–5
The Plague of Fantasies (Žižek, S.) 94–5
playground memories 131

poems: *Aeneid* (Virgil) 34–5; Barbershop 116; Borne Bare 116–17; Breathing 115; Carry-Out 117; Critical Qualitative Inquiry 112; "Critical Qualitative Inquiry Is/as Love" (Ulmer, J.) 112; Fast Break 116; Fugue 115; Golden Hour 115; Greetings, Stranger 113–14; Homework 114; *Leaning: A Poetics of Personal Relations* (Pelias, R.J.), poem in 110; The Long Way 117; Paths 113; Sweet Home Sweet 114; Toward the Finite Home 114
poiesis 85; autoethnography and 8
polis 20
politics: personal as political 19; political practice 56; spaciality and 50
Pontius Pilate 15
post-structuralism 126
post-war writings 61
postmodern logics 25–6
poubellication 94–6
Poulos, Christopher 28, 72–3, 94, 108
privilege 42
project categorization 15–16
psychoanalysis 4, 35–6
psychotherapy, autoethnography and 4
publishing 61; published writing 102

qualitative inquiry 2, 3; critical qualitative inquiry 14–15, 19, 135; Critical Qualitative Inquiry (poem) 112; future for 21–3; *Qualitative Inquiry and Social Justice* (series) 14–18, 79; *Qualitative Inquiry* (journal) 79; qualitative methods as *poiesis* 34–5; social justice and 14–18; Western philosophy in 3
qualitative texts 119
quantum superposition, being-with and 69–71

rapport 129
reading autoethnography 7–13, 38
recklessness 55–7
relationships 10, 64, 77, 88; death to storytelling, relationship of 30; of desire 82; future relationships 20; grief in 102; home creation, desire towards 48; interpersonal relationships 19; intersubjective relationship 25; intimate relationships 89, 99–100; inverse proportionality and 64–5; lost relationships 103; loving relationships 89, 133; meaningful relationships 87,

109–10; of opposition 64; originary relationship 82; romantic relationships 19, 82; shame in 97; synchronic relationships 111–12; tripartite relationship 84; work relationships 129
reproductive health 18
research, importance of (or not) 61–3
respect 80–81; perspective and 81–2
Richardson, L. and St. Pierre, E.A. 134
rights-based projects 17–18
romantic relationships 19, 82
rules of home 73–4

Schmitt, Carl 44
scholarly community 121
scholarly writing 36, 38, 120
scholarship 119, 121; capitalist production and 125
Schreber, Daniel Paul 36
Schulman, Mort 76–7
Seattle 128
Selected Writings, Volume 2 (Benjamin, W.) 107
Selected Writings, Volume I (Benjamin, W.) 35
self-definition 24
self-organizing systems 125
self-reflection, being-with and 110
self-surveillance, gaze of 86–8
Seminar III (Lacan, J.) 65–6
Seminar V (Lacan, J.) 87–8
Seminar XI (Lacan, J.) 12, 67, 94
Seminar XX (Lacan, J.) 84
settler colonialism 17
shame: being excremental and 94; in relationships 97; shame sells 99–101; shameful writing 97; of stigma 96–7
Shane (George Stevens film) 79
sharing 101–3
signifiers 13, 81–2, 101–2, 111, 121, 133; in textual situations and autoethnography 12
silence: autoethnography as resistance to 26–7; between letters 121
"Single Ladies" (Beyoncé) 85–6
smacking 65–6
social justice: ethical framework for 14–15, 17–18; qualitative inquiry and 14–18
social media 118
"A Song for You/Killing Me Softly" (Alexander, B.K.) 82–4
songwriting 69; love and 82–4; unfinished love songs 84–6

space: space-time continuum 122; spatial arrangements 44; spatial distance 24; three-dimensional space 20
Sparks, Nicholas 37
Speedy, Jane 4
"Spirited Accidents" (Poulos, C.) 94
sports 127
Spry, Tami 10–11
Stigma: Notes on Management of Spoiled Identity (Goffman, E.) 96–7
stigma, shame of 96–7
"A Story Located in 'Shoulds'" (Pelias, R.J.) 21, 25, 32, 41, 60–61
strangers, welcomes for 43–4
stream-of-consciousness writing 120
stuckness 127, 128
Suber, Peter 95, 96
subversive power of autoethnography 97
suffering 66–7; distribution of 41–2
"Suffering Happiness" (Bochner, A.P.) 64–5
superego imperative 127
supplementation 5
Supreme Court 15
surveillance 131
Sutton, Timothy Matthew Lee 102–3
synchronic relationships 111–12

Tamas, Sophie 88–90
taxonomization 8–9
technique of writing 35
"Tell Me Something Good" (Chaka Khan song) 2
temporal determination 75
"Notes on Terrible Educations" (Hill, D.C. at al.) 57
textual analysis 4
TGI Fridays 122–3
theory: theorists and 126; theorization about autoethnography 9–10
thinking: fairness in 17; is/as of writing and 121; technology, thinkings about 62; through writing 120–21, 122; writing as 120, 122, 134
A Thousand Plateaus (Guattari, F. and Deleuze, G.) 129
"Throughness" (Carless, D.) 69
thrownness 48, 51
thyme, sage advice about 107–8
time 39–40; being-with and 91, 110–12; at home 47–8; itinerary time 72; movement through 42–3; slow time of home 105–6; temporal determination

75; world time as time of method 71–2; writing about shared time 111
togetherness 23–6
Transgender Psychoanalysis (Gherovici, P.) 55
tripartite relationship 84
tritanopia 134
truth in autoethnography: forces of 72–4; pain of closure of 76–7
Tuck, Eve 15–17
"Turning Toward Tincup: A Story of a Home Death" (Hocker, J.) 29–30

Ulmer, Jasmine B. 2, 3, 71, 112; from James to (online communications) 118, 119–22, 122–4, 124–5, 126, 127–9, 129–32, 132–3, 134–5
unconscious 128
unfairness 19, 50; home in unfair world, justice and 50–53
universe pooling 135
The Unnameable (Beckett, S.) 123
unsaid, existence of 123
"Useless Suffering" (Levinas, E.) 66–7
utilitarianism 14–15

value of: autoethnography 4–5; method 33–4
Virgil 34–5
vulnerability 97–9; subversion by wilfull exposure of 99–101
"The Vulnerable Academic" (Bhattacharya, K.) 45–6

Waiting for Godot (Samuel Beckett play) 123
walls 123, 126

Waters, Hill L. 57
way of life, autoethnography as 13
"The Way We Weren't" (Harris, A.) 76–7
"The Wedding Dress" (Giorgio, G.) 104
"What Is Peace?" (Kavoori, A.) 44–5
"Where the Wild Dreams Are" (Speedy, J.) 4
windows 39–40
work relationships 129
world time as time of method 71–2
writing 5, 9–10, 12, 25–6, 32, 35–6, 41, 57, 76–7, 85, 88, 94, 118; about autoethnography 8–9, 13; about emotion 78–9; about shared time 111; autoethnography 7, 11, 13, 25, 26–7, 35, 101, 103; being-with and 11–12, 33; called autoethnography 4–5, 7; collaborative writing groups 88; is thinking 120, 122, 134; letter writing 118–35; literary reviews and 37; post-war writings 61; published writing 102; scholarly writing 36, 38, 120; shameful writing 97; songwriting 69; stream-of-consciousness writing 120; technique of 35; to thinking, is/as of 121; thinking through 120–21, 122
Wyatt, Jonathan 88–90

Yang, K. Wayne 15–17
Yoo, Joanne 105
"You're Going to Do What?" (Forber-Pratt, A.J.) 27

Zeno's paradox of motion 75
Žižek, Slavoj 61–2, 94–5, 95–6